GUNS UNDER MY CHINAR

GUNS UNDER MY CHINAR

KASHMIR'S COVERT WARS

A.M. WATALI

RUPA

Published by
Rupa Publications India Pvt. Ltd 2024
7/16, Ansari Road, Daryaganj
New Delhi 110002

Sales centres:
Bengaluru Chennai Hyderabad
Jaipur Kathmandu Kolkata
Mumbai Prayagraj

The views and opinions expressed in this book are the author's own and the facts are as reported by him, which have been verified to the extent possible, and the publishers are not in any way liable for the same.

P-ISBN: 978-93-5702-981-0
E-ISBN: 978-93-5702-743-4

First impression 2024

10 9 8 7 6 5 4 3 2 1

Printed in India

To
my soulmate, my late wife Atiqua;

our children, Mushtaq, Shafqat, Massarat and Asgar;
our daughters-in-law
Hussan Ara, Zainab Shamas and Azra
and our son-in-law Khurshid,
who brought light into our lives
our grandchildren Omar, Haseeb, Nazli, Nawal, Osman,
Azaan, Hajra and Dildaar,
who made our world happier and filled it with warmth.

To my senior and junior colleagues in
the Jammu & Kashmir Police,
who never let me down while these stories came to life.

Lastly, to the common people of my state,
who always reposed great confidence in me.

Contents

Introduction

My stories are about the relentless efforts of the state police to contain the ever-rising trajectory of the resistance movement, backed by Pakistani intelligence agencies, and manage the fragile peace in Kashmir over a period of four decades (1947–89). Despite our efforts, the resistance has continued to loom on the horizon, mostly because of the alienation of the youth for one reason or another. Absolute peace cannot be achieved without a final solution regarding the Kashmir dispute between India and Pakistan, in accordance with people's aspirations.

Instead of carrying this historical testimony to my grave, my purpose is to leave behind an authentic record of the significant happenings during this crucial period for posterity. I feel duty-bound to truthfully reveal everything within my knowledge without prejudice or ideological bias. I hope my critics too will view this work positively and appreciate my contribution to preserving critical historical material. These biographical stories drawn from my memory are woven into an episodic thread for the readers' convenience.

Chapter 1

Trajectory of Resistance

BOMBS NEXT DOOR

I remember the autumn of 1948 when I was in Handwara market, in my home town, after arriving from Srinagar, where I was an intermediate class student of Sri Pratap College (SP College). While watching the golden skyline after sunset, my attention was suddenly drawn to a couple of speeding jeeps overflowing with men in civvies and uniform. The jeeps sped towards the western part of the town and disappeared into a cloud of dust on the unmetalled road. All the shopkeepers and others present in the market wondered about this unusual movement of policemen in jeeps towards the border area of Rajwar. The jeeps reportedly returned after nightfall and had sped off towards Srinagar without stopping at Handwara.

The next day, when the locals of Rajwar came to the market, a rumour spread that the Special Staff (SS) of the police, headed by Sheikh Ghulam Qadir Ganderbali, had raided the premises of the rajas of Zachaldara and Rajpora—the jagirdars (feudatories of the Maharaja). The rumour suggested that the SS had uncovered bombs concealed beneath the harvested paddy stalks belonging to the rajas. It was the first time I heard of bombs being discovered in our neighbourhood, only about 4 km from our residence. I faintly comprehended that the recovery of bombs had something to do with the ongoing Indo-Pak war.

Raja Inayatullah Khan, his brother Raja Habibullah Khan of Zachaldara and several other rajas from Rajpora had been arrested by the SS during the raid. However, Raja Ehsaanullah Khan of Rajpora had given the slip to the SS sleuths. With the help of a local guide, Akbar, he reportedly crossed over to Pakistan-occupied Kashmir (PoK) via the Bungus Valley, where he settled down for the rest of his life. Several people, including Master Ghulam Ahmed (Abdul Ghani Lone's mentor and later his father-in-law), were arrested. Subsequently, I came to know that one of my very able and dedicated teachers at Government High School, Handwara, Ghulam Hassan Ganai, a resident of Ganapora, Langate, had also been arrested. This case came to be known as the 'Srinagar Bomb Case'.

It was also rumoured that the bombs were supplied from across the border by Pakistani secret agencies to fuel sabotage and subversion in the Valley. Many years later, in the early 1960s, Abdul Ghani Lone (who was a prominent leader of the state), belonging to the backward village of Harai in the border area of Kupwara, told me that during those times, he was a schoolboy living with the family of Master Ghulam Ahmed at Sopore, who provided him free boarding and lodging to facilitate his studies at a local high school. In those days, many generous and philanthropic city and town dwellers provided such facilities to poor students hailing from remote rural areas to enable their studies in high schools and colleges. Lone told me that because he lived with the family, he was also arrested and interrogated in connection with the bomb case but was not charged.

'However, it would be incorrect to say that Pakistan had no sympathizers here'.[1] Even before the Indian Army was stationed in Kashmir, a substantial portion of the state's population, including

---

[1]Abdullah, Sheikh Mohammad, *The Blazing Chinar: An Autobiography*, Gulshan Books, Srinagar, 2013, 311.

the Muslim population of Jammu, aspired for the state's accession to Pakistan. However, the majority preferred independence as envisaged in the Naya Kashmir Resolution of the National Conference (NC) passed in 1944. Prior to the tribal raid of 1947, a pro-Pakistan students' outfit had already been formed under the name and style of the Pakistan Students' Federation with Mohammad Shafi Qureshi as its president and an office in present-day Badshah Chowk, Srinagar. Ironically, it was Qureshi who established the Indian National Congress in Kashmir during the Bakshi regime. Later, he became India's railway minister and held some gubernatorial assignments before his death.

Post accession, the first pro-Pakistan demonstrations marked by slogans of 'Pakistan Zindabad' were held in the presence of the United Nations Security Council (UNSC) commission at Sri Pratap College, Srinagar, in 1948. These latent sentiments resurfaced in 1952 with the establishment of the Political Conference by Ghulam Mohi-ud-Din Kara, a hardcore senior leader of the NC. Revolting against his own party, Kara announced the formation of the Political Conference during a public meeting in downtown Sehyaar Aali Kadal, Srinagar. After the formation of the new party, he asked people to openly express their choice. The audience unanimously shouted, 'We want Pakistan'. With the passage of time, these sentiments curved the trajectory of resistance steeply upwards, which at no stage could be crushed.

After the tribal raiders were pushed back from Shalateng, a neighbourhood in Srinagar, a group of local pro-Pakistan elements formed an underground organization in or around 1948 to carry out anti-India political activities and initiate covert acts of sabotage and subversion. Some active members of the pro-Pakistan Jammu and Kashmir Muslim Conference (JKMC) joined hands with some deserters from the state army (now Jammu and Kashmir Rifles) and the Maharaja's army, who had mutinied in the wake of the armed uprising in Mirpur, Poonch and adjoining areas.[2] A few of them had also joined the tribal raiders, who attacked the state from the Valley's western border. The headquarters of this underground outfit was established at Poonch in PoK under Captain Mannan.

The prominent founding members of the JKMC included Captain Mannan of the state army, Jahangir Khan, his brother Alamgir Khan, Mohammad Iqbal Bhat (later a minister in PoK), Ghulam Naqi, Mohammad Rafiq Shahmiri, Muhammad Aslam Khan—a retired British Army officer and the eldest son of Brigadier Rehmatullah Khan—Haji Jalal-ud-Din of Charar-e-Sharief, Abdul Rahim Waza, Raja Feroz Khan, Raja Attaullah Khan, Inayatullah Kakroo of Baramulla, Dr Abdul Majid of Anantnag, Raja Inayatullah and Raja Habibullah of Zachaldara (Handwara).[3] Most members of the pro-Pakistan underground cells were feudal landlords and officers of the state army. Some of them, who were the cream of the middle-rung leadership of the Muslim Conference, continued living in the state even after the senior leaders migrated to Pakistan.

Meanwhile, Raja Attaullah, who had allegedly established contacts with Pakistani intelligence authorities, smuggled pony loads of Sten guns (carbines), revolvers and ammunition from PoK into the Valley via secret border routes in collaboration with Jahangir Khan, Mohammad Iqbal Bhat and Mir Abdul Rashid.[4] Additionally, records show that 700 bombs, allegedly buried in Brigadier Rehmatullah Khan's (father of Air Marshal Asghar Khan of Pakistan) orchard at Bagh-e-Mehtab, Srinagar, were uncovered by the SS, following disclosures made by the Brigadier's servant

---

[2]Saraf, Muhammad Yusuf, *Kashmiris Fight for Freedom, Vol. 2 (1947–1978)*, Ferozsons, Lahore, 1979, 547.

[3]Ibid. 1192–1194.

[4]Ibid.

during interrogation. Numerous members of the underground organization were arrested during Sheikh Abdullah's regime but on their release, many of them, including Brigadier Rehmatullah Khan, crossed over to Pakistan. Some of the migrated lot, such as Abdul Rahim Waza, returned to resettle in India with the permission of Sheikh Abdullah and his Deputy Prime Minister (Home) Bakshi Ghulam Mohammad. Ganderbali also helped many resettle. A prominent businessman, Waza died in the early 1990s. A great friend of mine, he was a great asset to the administration and always helped with the maintenance of peace.

Inayatullah Kakroo, a well-known businessman and senior leader of the Muslim Conference, had reportedly collaborated with the tribal raiders actively during their occupation of Baramulla, so much so that his home was the headquarters of Peer Manki Sharief, the raiders' spiritual head. Ironically, after Peer Manki's departure, the retreating tribal raiders looted valuables from Kakroo's house also. Kakroo, however, did not cross over to Pakistan. He was arrested, and after his release, he re-established his business in Baramulla, where he already had an established cinema hall. All along, Kakroo maintained cordial relations with pro-India politicians and officials; I personally witnessed senior officers of the Indian Army stationed there enjoying his hospitality on several occasions during my posting as the Senior Superintendent of Police (SSP) in Baramulla, after the 1971 war. Others who were part of the pro-Pakistan movement, such as Dr Mustafa Shah, brother of Mubarak Shah of Baramulla (a senior NC leader and minister) and Colonel Dr Abdul Majid Mir of Pampore (brother of Ghulam Mohammad Mir Tawoos of Pampore, who was the home secretary of the state during Sadiq's tenure) migrated to and settled in Pakistan.

Back to the Srinagar Bomb Case. During the investigation, numerous people were arrested and interrogated, including

Haji Jalal-ud-Din who was transferred to Red Fort in Delhi for 'specialized interrogation'. He reportedly did not disclose anything self-incriminating to his interrogators, especially about the disposal of arms smuggled into the Valley from PoK on ponies. However, Mohammad Iqbal Bhat, Mir Abdul Rashid, Ghulam Qadir Bhat, Ali Mohammad Mir and Ghulam Naqi were put on trial. Jahangir Khan was declared a proclaimed offender. Notably, two of the convicts, Ali Mohammad Mir of Basant Bagh and Ghulam Naqi of Alamgari Bazaar, Srinagar, managed to escape in April 1951 and crossed over to Pakistan.

This informal underground organization was also allegedly responsible for setting public properties like dak bungalows, vital bridges, culverts, etc. on fire. One such case was known as the Akkad Case, which involved the burning of Maharaja Hari Singh's fishing lodge in Akkad village near Aishmuqam on the banks of the Lidder Nalla. The accused were Dr Abdul Majid and Advocates Ghulam Mohi-ud-Din Shawl, Ghulam Rasool Kochak and Ghulam Nabi Kochak from Anantnag. Following the arrest of Sheikh Mohammad Abdullah in 1953, all of them joined the Plebiscite Front (PF), a separatist organization formed by Mirza Afzal Beg in 1955. Later, following the Indira–Sheikh Accord of 1975, Shawl and Ghulam Rasool Kochak were elected as Members of Parliament while Ghulam Nabi Kochak became a cabinet minister of the state. Dr Majid served as the chairman of the local municipality. Unsurprisingly, Ghulam Nabi Kochak was one of the defectors when Dr Farooq Abdullah's government was unlawfully dismissed by Jagmohan in 1984. Deserters from the Maharaja's army, including Captain Allah Dad Khan, Lieutenant Ehsanullah and Lieutenant Ghulam Nabi Dar, were court-martialled and sentenced to long terms of imprisonment.[5]

---

[5]Saraf, Muhammad Yusuf, *Kashmiris Fight for Freedom, Vol. 2 (1947–1978)*, Ferozsons, Lahore, 1979.

AKBAR JASOOS

Though his name has been mentioned before as the guide who helped Raja Ehsanullah cross over to Pakistan, I would like to introduce Akbar as a spook. A resident of my neighbouring village, Bakhihakhar, Handwara, he came to be known as Akbar Jasoos. I never got to meet him as he went underground after the Srinagar Bomb Case came to light. Akbar may have been enlisted as a courier and spy by agencies on the other side. I had only heard stories of his so-called escapades crafted over the course of his ten-year tenure in the murky world of espionage. Some of the stories seemed to be only rumours, but by and large, what I am about to narrate is based on my personal knowledge.

Pakistani intelligence agencies may have been able to establish their espionage network in the Valley by collaborating with pro-Pakistan elements during the Indo-Pakistani War of 1947–48. Though he was illiterate, Akbar became a household name and legendary figure over time. He came to be identified not only as a notorious spy but also as a saboteur for allegedly burning down vital installations, including bridges, culverts and other assets like forest rest houses, tourist bungalows, etc. Subsequently, he reportedly became a trusted courier, transporting letters and cash for secret agents in the Valley and pro-Pakistan leaders. This made him the most wanted man by central agencies as well as the state police, particularly the SS headed by Sheikh Ghulam Qadir Ganderbali. However, Akbar was too clever to fall into any of their traps as he had intimate knowledge of the secret infiltration routes along the ceasefire line (CFL). He became a hardcore and dedicated Pakistani spy.

A story in common circulation was that on one of his secret forays into Srinagar, Akbar saw Ganderbali near the famous Mir Pan House on Residency Road, close to the Kothibagh Police

Station, which served as the headquarters of Ganderbali's Special Staff. While passing by, Akbar reportedly approached him and asked, 'What is the time by your watch?' It was a common query those days as only a few people could afford a watch. Ganderbali looked at his watch and told Akbar the time without getting the least suspicious. After a few days, Akbar was said to have boastfully broadcasted this incident on Azad Kashmir Radio, Trarkhal, in PoK. Though many such stories were attributed to Akbar, it is undisputed that he possessed the remarkable ability to cross the CFL undetected and at his discretion to execute subversive activities and acts of sabotage across the northern part of the Valley.

As time passed, I continued my education at SP College, Amar Singh College, Srinagar, and later at another university for my postgraduation in political science and LLB. Upon my return, I joined the Bar in Handwara and practised for a few years before being appointed as a Government Prosecutor at Anantnag. In 1958, following my mother's death, I was reassigned to Handwara on compassionate grounds with the intervention of none other than Bakshi Ghulam Mohammad, the then prime minister of Jammu and Kashmir, who knew my father and uncle as freedom fighters. Suddenly, I was told about Akbar's arrest in the Bungus Valley near the CFL. The whole operation was purportedly carried out by a Sikh gentleman—a junior-level officer of the Intelligence Bureau (IB) posted at Handwara. This story seemed unbelievable and dubious as nobody could navigate the wilderness of the thick forests and lush green meadows of Bungus alone, that too so close to the CFL. Neither was the local police taken into confidence nor was a claim made of any assistance taken from the troops guarding the CFL. I knew the Sikh gentleman very well. In retrospect, given my personal experience of about 40 years in the field, I guess that Akbar, fed up with this life of stress and strain, must have negotiated his surrender through his relatives back home. Another possibility is that the IB officer may have taken the initiative and persuaded Akbar's family for his surrender, a tactic not uncommon in such professions. Whatever the reality, it was the end of Akbar Jasoos's covert career.

The IB officer further claimed to have seized a copy of the Holy Quran from Akbar's possession. He showcased the sacred scripture, which, according to him, contained hundred-rupee Indian currency notes amounting to ₹10,000 concealed within its hardbound covers. Without separating the double hardcovers with a sharp knife or blade, the money could not be detected. The IB officer also showed two plain white paper sheets that had allegedly been used to cover the notes, claiming that they were actually letters written in invisible ink. The text of the letter could not be read with the naked eye without scientific aid from a forensic science laboratory. Surprisingly, the IB officer revealed the pinkish writing by rubbing a candle on the blank sheets. Being a young, untrained and inexperienced person, I watched the whole affair very inquisitively. It was a top secret affair shared only with me and the station house officer (SHO). According to the IB officer, Akbar had confessed that the amount was meant to be delivered to the wife of a jailed senior pro-Pakistan leader. I did not pursue the matter further but came to know that Akbar was not prosecuted in any court. He was soon moved to some unknown destination.

After a few years in jail, Akbar was released and he settled in his village, Bakhihakhar, in my neighbourhood. He resumed a normal life and my father helped him in his rehabilitation as a neighbour. Time passed and during one of my visits home, I found a middle-aged person sitting with my father in the verandah. He was introduced to me as Akbar Jasoos. I was excited to meet the legendary spy sitting in front of me and eager to hear some sensational stories of his life as a spy. Akbar disclosed the story of the selfish wife of an incarcerated politician, for whom he had brought money from a Pakistani agency at great risk to his life. According to him, he reached the politician's house around sunset to deliver the money to his wife. Upon receiving the amount, she asked Akbar to leave immediately because she feared a police raid on her house. Akbar told her that it was dangerous for him to leave at such late hour and requested her to accommodate him in her house for the night. The lady refused despite his entreaties. She even refused him entry into the house, leading to an arguement. Akbar did not budge and was determined to stay there as he was worried that he would be arrested if he stayed in some mosque or some other public space. Ultimately, instead of allowing him into her palatial house, the lady permitted him to stay on a tree in her lawn. Akbar climbed the tree and stayed there through the night. Before dawn, he got down and left.

Given his advanced age, Akbar did not engage in any anti-national or subversive activities following his release. However, with the mass uprising of the youth in the early 1990s and the subsequent opening of the Line of Control (LoC) after the appointment of Jagmohan as governor for a second time, Akbar found himself drawn back into the world of espionage. He volunteered to guide a group of youth across the LoC via the Bungus–Lipa Valley route. Destiny played a tragic role when Akbar and his group were noticed by the army somewhere near the LoC. The army fired and reportedly killed all of them, including our legendary Akbar Jasoos. According to my assessment, Akbar lost his life because he took an uncommon route for those days. Dumari Gali in the north was the only safe route used by Kashmiri youth; they were even allowed free passage by the security forces in the early 1990s. Nevertheless, Akbar laid down his life, proving his commitment to the profession he had taken up as early as 1947–48.

JAHANGIR KHAN

In Srinagar, there was an underground cell headed by Jahangir Khan, a resident of Bagh-e-Mehtab on the outskirts of Srinagar. Jahangir Khan, a well-to-do orchardist, was a passionate pro-Pakistani. He had proved to be an important asset to tribal raiders and accompanying Pakistani officers, to the extent that he voluntarily acted as their guide when they reached Badgam in 1947 in a bid to capture Srinagar airport. Later, he was said to have been engaged for a long time by Pakistani intelligence authorities in their covert espionage activities as well as for organizing subversion and sabotage within the Valley. He was suspected to have been trained by Pakistani intelligence authorities as a trainer in the use of arms and explosives. Eluding arrest, Jahangir Khan dedicatedly continued his covert espionage activities for about three decades. Jahangir Khan remained on the state's subversive scene for several decades, and continued to be in the 'line of fire' of the state police for some decades without achieving any success.

It may be recalled that Jahangir Khan was actively involved in smuggling loads of arms, ammunition, etc. into the Valley in 1948 in collaboration with some people of an underground outfit. He was also an absconding accused and proclaimed offender in the Kashmir Conspiracy Case lodged against Sheikh Mohammad Abdullah, Mirza Afzal Beg, Begum Abdullah and other leaders. Finally, Jahangir was arrested in Poonch in 1961. He faced trial before the Special Court until the case was withdrawn post-1965. Instead of being released, he was re-arrested and put on trial for the Srinagar Bomb Case of 1948 as a proclaimed offender. As the case was very old, no evidence was available. By that time, all the witnesses had passed away and no charges could be sustained against him. He was acquitted and released in 1968. Following his release, he settled in Haka Khal, a hilly village in the Beerwah area of present-day Badgam district. He started a poultry farm there, which later proved to be only a cover for his renewed clandestine activities.

THE COUP

Following the dismissal and arrest of Prime Minister Sheikh Mohammad Abdullah, the resistance movement, which was in its infancy, became institutionalized with the establishment of the PF in 1955 by Mirza Mohammad Afzal Beg under the patronization of Sheikh Mohammad Abdullah. The PF was the first separatist outfit to demand the implementation of UNSC resolutions for conducting a plebiscite to ascertain the will of the people for the accession of the state to either India or Pakistan. With Sheikh's arrest, the alienation of the people, particularly the youth, escalated limitlessly. The majority who favoured accession to India became hostile overnight because of Sheikh's unlawful arrest and dismissal. It is on record that even as a student, Maqbool Ahmed Bhat (later hanged in Tihar Jail), who has now become an icon of 'Azadi', was greatly influenced by Sheikh's leadership and ideology.

It is a well-known fact that Sheikh chose to align with India instead of Pakistan due to ideological reasons. In spite of Kashmir being a Muslim-majority state and geographically close to Pakistan, he opted to remain with secular India, influencing his people with his ideology. However, when Nehru's actions led to Sheikh's arrest, it understandably resulted in a shift in sentiment among the people, causing them to turn against India.

Notwithstanding the arrest of PF leaders and its workers from time to time, the PF rose to become a vibrant and popular organization demanding a plebiscite as per the UN resolution. The misguided and short-sighted policy of Jawaharlal Nehru, aimed at stabilizing his own threatened throne due to the agitation in Jammu by communal forces, had its fallout in some areas of neighbouring Punjab. Instead of facing such forces, he preferred to appease them by removing Sheikh Abdullah. This Himalayan blunder infused new vitality into the resistance. Although the PF leadership was behind bars, the grassroots party workers carried out their programme throughout the length and breadth of the state.

Initially, the youth supported the PF's peaceful struggle but eventually they drifted towards the ideology of armed resistance. They formed small underground cells for subversion and sabotage. Politically, the masses continued to sympathize with and support the PF, recognizing Sheikh Abdullah as their only leader. By 1964–65, the non-violent struggle led by the incarcerated Sheikh Mohammad Abdullah and Mirza Afzal Beg lost its appeal among the youth. The baton of the resistance was taken over from the ageing leadership by students and youth. Additionally, Kashmiris, particularly the youth, were hugely influenced and inspired by the infiltrating Pakistani Mujahideen (regular troops) in 1965. That was an added reason for Kashmiri youth to strive for an armed struggle for freedom. Since there was no unifying leadership to take forward an armed movement, the youth formed micro underground cells but without any cohesive organizational set-up or coordination. To show their solidarity with the retreating Pakistani infiltrators, some underground outfits rendered all possible logistical and other help to them.

Nevertheless, the underground armed movement had yet to

take off, and the majority of the youth and students continued to express their anger and alienation through violent demonstrations and strikes. Disturbances were created on one pretext or another at the drop of a hat. The youth would resort to violence even for non-issues that were not necessarily connected to the conflict. The Palestinian cause, blasphemous contents of any book, Pakistan Day celebrations, Pakistan–India cricket matches, etc. posed serious law and order problems in the state. It was almost a daily affair for the police to deal with such violent mobs. Therefore, we, in the police, had to be on high alert every hour of the day. We could not afford to be complacent at any cost.

RED KASHMIR

To commence my narration of the violent phase, I will begin with the role of a young man named Ghulam Rasool Zahgir, a resident of Dabtal in downtown Srinagar. Zahgir will be one of the most important characters in some of my stories. A college dropout, Zahgir had a high level of commitment to the pro-Pakistan ideology, along with leadership qualities. He possessed strong convincing power and was able to enlist the support of the youth for his underground movement. Zahgir did not stick to any job or profession—he always displayed a restless passion to get rid of Indian rule by violent means. Like many other youngsters, he was greatly impressed by Operation Gibraltar initiated by Pakistan in August 1965 and the sacrifices of the Pakistani Mujahideen who infiltrated the state. However, Zahgir first drew adverse attention from police authorities when he was a clerk at Kashmir University, where he had allegedly put up posters preaching jihad against India. He was arrested in October 1965 and released in January 1966 as no serious charges were pressed against him.

After his release, Zahgir contacted other like-minded youth, some of whom were already sponsors of one or the other underground outfit or members of small underground cells. Syed Sarwar, a resident of Dabtal and Zahgir's neighbour, was the first to be contacted by him. Syed Sarwar was already heading his own small underground group called the Students' Revolutionary Council (SRC) with Ghulam Nabi Hajam, Mohammad Ashraf Baba and Abdul Hamid Shah as its members. Under Zahgir's influence, the SRC drew up plans for assassination, arson and other types of subversive sabotage aimed at igniting a public uprising against India. Initially, Zahgir had clandestinely brought out enigmatic cyclostyled posters titled 'Red Kashmir'. The title was quite misleading and mysterious as it could be attributed to any leftist party or a wing of the Communist Party preaching violence and bloodshed. These Red Kashmir posters were not only pasted on the city walls, poles, etc. but also mailed to political leaders, government officers, prominent businessmen and some private individuals, creating alarm in some parts of the state, particularly in Srinagar. The posters advocated for the liberation of Jammu and Kashmir from India and portrayed a map of India wherein Kashmir was an independent country, marked in red ink, contradicting Zahgir's pro-Pakistan ideology.

One of Zahgir's important associates, Fazal Haq Qureshi met him for the first time in Central Jail, Srinagar. Although Fazal was a government servant working in the finance department of the secretariat, he was ideologically a hardcore supporter of the state's accession to Pakistan. He had been detained by counterintelligence (CI) authorities for circulating posters under the banner of Mujahideen Mahaz-e-Azadi—an underground organization—that contained material prejudicial to the security of the state and maintenance of public order. Fazal was released in 1966. Once out of jail, he came in contact with Nazir Ahmed Wani, a junior agriculture officer in the state government. A resident of Tarabal, Eidgah, Srinagar, Nazir too was hardcore pro-Pakistan. Both of them had planned to organize the youth on violent lines. While their plans were still in discussion stage, they were contacted by Zahgir who inducted them into the Red Kashmir underground cell, where they were also introduced to Syed Sarwar and other members of the SRC.

ROOTS OF INSURGENCY

By December 1966, Zahgir had decided to carry out a sensational act intended to not only cause fear and panic among the people but also demoralize the police and security forces of the Government of India (GoI) in the state. Though various plans were discussed by him with members of his underground network, they ultimately decided to kill the Border Security Force (BSF) sentry guarding one of the bridges on the river Jhelum in downtown Srinagar. All seven members of Zahgir's underground outfit were part of this maiden operation. However, the mission was allegedly actually executed only by Zahgir and Syed Sarwar.

On the night of 3 February 1967, both of them attacked the sentry at Nawa Kadal Bridge on the river Jhelum with daggers, inflicting serious injuries to his chest. His .303 rifle along with five loaded rounds were also taken away. The injured sentry, Charan Dass, crawled some distance before dying. This was the first militant action by a small group in the violent resistance history of the state; it marked a paradigm shift from the peaceful struggle of the PF to the violent demonstrations of students and youth and low-level armed rebellion. The group claimed responsibility for the action in the next issue of Red Kashmir. With the killing of Charan Dass, the covert war became a more violent movement. Though a case was registered by the concerned police, no evidence was found by them. Ironically, without an iota of suspicion about his involvement in the murder of Charan Dass, the police detained Zahgir again under the Defence of India Rules to prevent him from acting in any manner prejudicial to the security of the state. Even during his arrest and detention, he was never suspected of being involved in Charan Dass's murder.

COLLABORATION WITH PAKISTAN

Fearing arrest, Nazir Ahmed Wani and Syed Sarwar crossed over to PoK in September 1967 from the northern part of the CFL with the help of a guide from Bandipore. In their absence, Fazal Haq continued to keep the Red Kashmir cell active. Reportedly, they both came into contact with Pakistani army officers Major Habibullah, Major Kaiser Qureshi and Major Tufail. Later, they also met the officers' superior, Brigadier Asghar. Nazir and Syed Sarwar were trained not only in the handling of arms and explosives but also in espionage techniques, intelligence gathering, organizing subversion and sabotage. Lessons were also imparted to them in self-security, evading surveillance, etc. Pakistani security officers instructed them to recruit as many Kashmiri youth as they could and send them for training in small groups.

In November 1967, their return journey was facilitated by Major Nazir Malik through the Sialkot–Ramgarh border in Jammu, with the aid of Abdul Rahman, aka Gurdial, a Sialkot-based guide. On their return, they recruited more young men, but only three, namely, Mohammad Ashraf Manhas from Shaheed Gunj, Iftikhar Paul from Aabi Guzar and Sahibzada Mohammad Amin of Malikyar, Srinagar, were sent to Pakistan via Jammu's Ramgarh border for training. Mohammad Ashraf Manhas, a government employee in the state secretariat, received special training in espionage and creating unrest by organizing strikes of government employees in a bid to disrupt the state administration. Manhas had allegedly played a prominent role in the government employees' strike in November 1967, which almost paralysed the Sadiq government.

Zahgir was released from jail in April 1968, with authorities blissfully unaware of his involvement in Charan Dass's murder. He immediately resumed the activities of Red Kashmir. Nazir Wani briefed him about his Pakistan visit in July 1968. Receiving a positive response from Pakistani security authorities, Zahgir and Nazir were encouraged to visit Pakistan through the Ramgarh–Sialkot border in Jammu. Both received training and instructions from army officers Colonel Bashir and Major Tufail. During this visit, they also met Brigadier Asghar and were introduced to Zafar Iqbal Rathore, a Pakistan Intelligence Bureau officer. The officials briefed them about their future roles and instructed them to build a strong underground outfit of committed youth for organized armed guerrilla activities. They were also asked to visit again for a more comprehensive and intensive briefing and training for a longer period. Meanwhile, they were asked to keep sending small batches of Kashmiri youth for training. Both of them returned through the same Ramgarh–Jammu route with the help of the Sialkot guide Gurdial. On his return, Zahgir disclosed details about a consignment of pencil bombs brought from Pakistan to some members of his outfit. To boost their morale, he even displayed a few pieces to them.

Nazir and Zahgir stepped up the recruitment of committed youth. Two significant individuals, Mohammad Aslam Wani of Zaldagar, Srinagar, and Zahoor Ahmed Shahdad of Bulbul Lanker, Srinagar, were recruited by them. This duo had already formed an underground outfit of their own, along with a few others. They had stolen National Cadet Corps (NCC) uniforms from Gandhi Memorial College situated in Bagh-i-Dilawar Khan in downtown Srinagar for their future operations. Their outfit had already attempted a dacoity at Islamia College to loot the armoury of dummy rifles for training. The group sent for the Islamia College operation had donned the NCC uniforms. On finding the chowkidar alert on duty, they attacked him with a dagger. The chowkidar raised an alarm that alerted two night-patrol police constables present in the area, who rushed to the college and succeeded in catching one attacker, Ghulam Mohammad Baba, a student of Gandhi Memorial College.

During investigations by CI sleuths, the names of many important underground outfits surfaced along with those of covert activists like Zahgir, Syed Sarwar, Nazir Ahmed Wani, Fazal Haq Qureshi, Saleem Beg and Mussadiq Hussain, who were identified as the brains behind the Islamia College armoury dacoity. Syed Sarwar was arrested in Delhi. With his arrest, the BSF sentry's murder case was also solved. However, by that time, the ring leaders, Zahgir, Fazal Haq and Mussadiq, had crossed over to Pakistan. Nazir Ahmed Wani went to Delhi to evade arrest, where he allegedly met Pakistan High Commission (PHC) officials and sought their advice. Reportedly, the PHC officials told him to return to the Valley and make efforts to reassemble all the members of his outfit to continue the assigned tasks.

We will meet these characters again in a separate chapter.

MASTER CELL

Around 1964, unaware of the activities of the individuals mentioned in the previous sections, another important underground cell had been formed independently by Mian Ghulam Sarwar, a college dropout and son of Mian Ghulam Mohammad, a local bureaucrat. Christened 'Master Cell' by CI authorities, the other prominent members of the cell were Zafar

Ahmed Kuttay, son of another local bureaucrat, Mohammad Ashraf, son of a deputy secretary and nephew of Ghulam Ahmed, private secretary to the Chief Minister (CM) G.M. Sadiq, Mohammad Ali Mir of Kishtwar and Bashir Ahmed Kichloo of Doda. All members, except Sarwar, were students of Regional Engineering College (REC) Hazratbal, Srinagar.

The formation of this cell was another serious effort by the youth to launch an armed struggle. Sarwar and his colleagues had also decided to acquire arms and ammunition from Pakistan. Accordingly, in 1964, two senior members, Mohammad Ali Mir and Bashir Ahmed Kichloo, were sent to Pakistan. Both of them crossed the CFL with the help of a paid guide. They convinced Pakistani intelligence and security officers that the time was ripe for armed struggle as the Kashmiri youth were ready to pick up arms against the Indian state. However they were not provided with any substantial arms aid except a rifle each and some explosives. They were also provided elementary training in handling arms. The Pakistani establishment actually planned to use the Master Cell for their 1965 Mujahideen expedition to incite a mass uprising in the Valley. By the time they returned, some more young men like Dr Abdul Hamid, a medical practitioner, Mohammad Yousseff Bhat, aka Mujahid, and Aijaz Rasool, both engineering students, and some others had joined the Master Cell. Aijaz was the son of the famous surgeon Dr Ghulam Rasool.

As the apex body, the Master Cell had a sort of loose control over some other underground cells, including the REC Cell headed by Mohammad Ashraf and the Narwara Cell headed by Mohammad Hussain, an engineer. Some hand grenades, which they had obtained from Pakistani infiltrators, were used in attacks at Regal Chowk, Maisuma and Medical College, Srinagar. According to CI sleuths, Dr Hamid had thrown the hand grenade at Regal Chowk, which caused injuries to some passers-by, while Aijaz Rasool and Zafar Kuttay had thrown grenades at Government Medical College and Maisuma (a crowded marketplace) respectively. However, while working on this book, I was told by one of the ex-members of the cell that the Maisuma grenade attack, in which some lives were lost, was carried out by one of the members of the Narwara Cell. Subsequently, the CI of the state dismantled the Master Cell and arrested most of its important members, barring Mohammad Ashraf and Bashir Ahmed Kichloo.

Meanwhile, most of the arrested members of the Master Cell had been arrested by the state's CI organization and detained under the Preventive Detention Act. In 1966, a handwritten letter on a dirty sheet was received in the state's Home Department with a copy of the order passed by Justice Subba Rao, the then Chief Justice of India (CJI). The letter was purportedly written from an unknown place of confinement in Jammu and Kashmir (J&K) by some members of the Master Cell. In view of the alarming contents, the CJI had directed the letter to be treated as a writ of habeas corpus and ordered the state government to physically present the prisoners before the court on the specified date. This letter, coupled with the court order, placed the state government in an awkward situation because the CJI's order created quite an alarm in the corridors of power, particularly in the state home department, as serious charges were levelled against the government, particularly against some CI officers. Furthermore, the act of smuggling out the letter was a serious security lapse.

In those days, I was looking after all the writ petitions filed against the state in the Supreme Court because of my legal background and work experience gained during the hearing of appeals, particularly in the matter of Bakshi Ghulam Mohammad. A commission of inquiry was appointed by the Sadiq government to inquire into the charges of corruption, amassing of huge assets and misuse of power by Bakshi and his family members. The commission was headed by Justice Ayyangar, a retired Supreme Court judge. I got an urgent call to attend a meeting at Home Minister Durga Prashad Dhar's Gupkar Road residence. Fondly known as DP, he was a dynamic person and an able administrator, possessing tremendous wit and courage. Moreover, he was a shrewd practitioner of covert statecraft. The meeting was also attended by the home secretary, the Inspector General of Police (IGP) of the state, Surendra Nath, as well as senior Crime Investigation Department (CID) officers.

The home minister briefly described the situation that had arisen because of the Supreme Court order, which was based on the letter smuggled out of a high-security detention centre in Bagh-e-Mehtab, Srinagar. The home minister directed me to assist the government in preparing a response and personally follow up on the matter in the Supreme Court. He also directed the concerned officers to inquire into the circumstances under which the letter was smuggled out and pinpoint the identity of the people involved. He directed the home department officials to make the relevant records available to me.

This was my initial encounter with the Master Cell, its activities and its leaders after having examined the records. The letter in question, addressed to the Hon'ble Chief Justice, was allegedly the brainchild of Mian Ghulam Sarwar, Zafar Kuttay, Dr Abdul Hamid and Mohammad Ali Mir, the prominent rebel leaders of the Master Cell who were detained in the Joint Interrogation Centre (JIC) of Bagh-e-Mehtab, Srinagar. They claimed that since their arrest and detention several months ago, they had not seen daylight, being continuously confined in a dark cell. They further informed the CJI that in the absence of any lighting in their cell, they were forced to write the letter by the moonlight that trickled into the room through a narrow aperture near the ceiling. They even expressed ignorance about the charges against them. Lastly, they claimed to have lost count of the number of days they had been confined.

I was presented with all the available documents like detention orders, grounds of detention, etc., which were prima facie technically defective. However, the discussion was deferred to a later meeting held after a few days. I was again called to the home department where I was handed a set of documents that included a government order declaring the Bagh-e-Mehtab Bungalow as a place of detention. The detention orders, grounds of detention and other connected records were all in order. I could only guess the power of the state apparatus.

A day before the date fixed by the Supreme Court, I flew to Delhi and escorted the detained young men in a very cordial atmosphere. I knew most of them. In Delhi, I handed them over to the SHO of the Parliament Street Police Station for transit custody. Besides contacting Government Advocate Dhebar of the central government that same evening, I also contacted M/s J.B. Dadachanji & Co. Advocates, the standing counsel for the state who had their office opposite the police station on Parliament Street. I knew the individuals at the firm well as I had closely worked with them from 1965 to 1969, not only in Bakshi's appeal matter but also in other matters of the state. Ravinder Narain and O.C. Mathur, the young advocates on record and partners of the firm, were good friends of mine. The case was assigned to Ravinder, who had worked on the Bakshi case with me. During the blackout in the 1965 war, he used to drive me to Kashmir House in the pitch dark every midnight without headlights. I briefed Ravinder about the facts of the case and passed on all the papers to him before leaving for Kashmir House, where I was staying.

The next morning, the detenus were produced before the

three-judge bench of the Supreme Court, presided over by Chief Justice Subba Rao. As soon as the case was called, Mian Sarwar got up and tried to present a small bottle containing flour allegedly contaminated with live worms, visible to the naked eye. He intended to demonstrate to the court the contaminated food they were served in jail. However, Ravinder got up and made preliminary submissions to draw the attention of the court to the merits of the case. The judges did not take any notice of the allegation made by Mian Sarwar. The CJI asked the detenus if they had a counsel or could engage one, to which they replied in the negative. Addressing the members of the bar present in the courtroom, the CJI asked them if anyone would volunteer to appear as amicus curiae for them. One advocate offered to represent them. The CJI directed him to file a regular writ of habeas corpus and adjourned the case, with the direction to keep the detenus in Tihar Jail pending the final disposal of the matter.

On Ravinder's suggestion, the state government engaged Nanabhoy (Nani) Ardeshir Palkhivala, a famous senior advocate practising in Bombay. He to frequently fly in from Bombay for Supreme Court hearings and stay at the Tata House on Prithviraj Road, as he was one of their directors. After the regular writ petition was filed for the detenus by the amicus curiae, return pleadings and affidavits were drafted by Ravinder, who sought an appointment with Palkhivala's office to settle the draft. The office informed Ravinder that Palkhivala would see him on his way to Palam from Tata House: 'You can accompany him in his car but he has fixed another "conference" with another counsel who will also be in the same car. He will settle your draft at the airport in the few minutes available before boarding.' That was how tight Palkhivala's schedule was. This also proved my law teacher Khawaja Mohammad Isaaq Sahib at Muslim University, Aligarh, right; in his farewell address, he told our batch, 'My dear boys, you are going into a profession that is overcrowded. But mind you, it is overcrowded at the bottom, not at the top.' How true!

Ravinder and I sat in the front seat of the Ambassador, next to the driver. Palkhivala and the other counsel were in the back seat discussing another case. As the driver pulled up in front of the Palam terminal, Palkhivala abruptly stopped talking, though the other counsel continued his presentation. Walking briskly into the terminal ahead of us, Palkhivala occupied a seat in the departure lounge. 'Come on, Ravinder. Show me the papers,' he asked Ravinder, who handed him the papers and sat down beside him. I took the seat across from them. He glanced through, shuffled the pages and said, 'It seems to be all right. As for the rest, let us see in court.' He wrote 'settled' and signed the draft. I don't mean to imply that Palkhivala was careless or casual in his profession. He may have read the relevant paragraph or two to comprehend the stand taken by the government. Once engaged, senior advocates do suggest a few points to be included in the reply or petition, as the case may be.

On the final day of the hearing, Palkhivala was at his best in terms of facts and the law. He seemed to have grasped all the nuances of the matter. Notwithstanding the allegations made by the detenus, their detention was declared valid under the law. Justice Subba Rao announced in the open court, 'Writ dismissed. Sorry, young men. This court could not help you.' Thus, the smuggled letter could not help the Master Cell masterminds and its members to get freedom because the state government, with all its resources, outsmarted them.

In due course, all the members of the Master Cell were released. They all resumed their studies (except Mian Sarwar) and settled down in their lives. Zafar Kuttay and Mohammad Yousseff Bhat retired as chief engineers. Dr Hamid practised medicine but died young. Mian Sarwar did not pursue any particular profession. At one point, he was following Maqbool Ahmed Bhat's appeal in the Supreme Court. Later, he was very close to Mufti Mohammad Sayeed for a long time. Mian Sarwar died a natural death, and I was told that his children are well settled because of their able upbringing by his wife.

SPY CHASE

Two members of the Master Cell, Mohammad Ashraf and Bashir Ahmed Kichloo, who had evaded arrest, developed contacts in the PHC in New Delhi. Both were allegedly used for espionage as well as to boost resistance. How Ashraf contacted the PHC is an interesting story, which he narrated to me before his death. Evading arrest, Ashraf went to Delhi to explore the possibility of getting an appointment with the High Commissioner of Pakistan even though he had never visited the PHC before. Arshad Hussain, the foreign minister in Bhutto's government, was the high commissioner. An intelligent guy, Ashraf chose not to visit the PHC at Chanakyapuri as he believed the place to be under the strict watch of the police and intelligence agencies. Therefore, he visited Arshad Hussain's residence at 6 Tilak Marg. The guard outside told him the high commissioner received visitors only at the high commission and not at his residence. Ashraf told him that he had come all the way from Kashmir and wanted to see the commissioner regarding an urgent matter. Initially, the guard denied him entry, but Ashraf persuaded him to deliver his visiting card to the high commissioner. After some time, the sentry returned and ushered Ashraf into the drawing room; he also cautioned Ashraf about the high commissioner's dinner engagement and advised him not to take more than 10–15 minutes. The sentry also advised him not to wait for the high commissioner to ask him to leave. Soon thereafter, Hussain joined him. Ashraf informed him about the situation in Kashmir and the progress made by the underground movement. After a few minutes, Ashraf abruptly stopped and got ready to leave as advised by the guard. However, Hussain asked him to continue and cancelled his dinner appointment.

Ashraf talked to him for over an hour. Later, Hussain summoned the first secretary, who arrived in no time along with his assistant. Coincidentally all three of them had the same name. Ashraf later learned that First Secretary Arshad was actually a police officer holding the rank of Deputy Inspector General (DIG) of Police and Raja Arshad, his assistant, was a superintendent of police (SP) in the Pakistan Police Service. The meeting at 6 Tilak Marg went on till midnight, in which all the plans for strengthening and assisting the underground movement were finalized. Hussain reportedly promised Ashraf help. Thereafter, Ashraf developed a strong bond with the Pakistan high commissioner. Ashraf and Bashir were given asylum in the PHC when the state CI was on the lookout to arrest them.

I was not involved in the investigation of the Master Cell or any other underground outfits initially. Stories about the secret cells shared in this book are based on the information derived from my colleagues in the CI and the report of Surendra Nath, IGP of the state, which he dictated in my presence in 1971. From 1965 to 1968, I was mostly engaged with the Ayyangar Commission set up by the Sadiq government to investigate the allegations against Bakshi Ghulam Mohammad. In between, I had a stint in the internal security section of the state home department, where I was responsible for overseeing the return and rehabilitation of migrant families from the Poonch and Rajouri areas who had strayed into PoK to save their lives and livestock from the vagaries of the 1965 war.

What I was now being asked to do was absolutely beyond my comprehension. Unexpectedly, I was being pushed into the dark alleys of espionage as a spy catcher. In hindsight, I feel like I was being groomed for a more responsible assignment in the executive police by my top bosses in the police hierarchy, who were keenly observing my performance. I remember D.P. Dhar once addressing me as 'our roving ambassador' because of my frequent travels in connection with the Bakshi case and other missions. Suddenly, one day in 1966, I received a call from Surendra Nath, then DIG CID, who handed me an inland letter. According to him, the letter had been seized from the house of an arrested student of REC related to Ashraf, who had gone underground. 'Please read it,' the CID chief told me. I couldn't make any sense of the contents. He told me that Ashraf, who had earlier been hiding in the PHC in New Delhi, had moved to Bombay (now Mumbai) where he was putting up with a Kashmiri business family related to him. 'I have decided to depute you to trace this boy in Bombay and arrest him,' the chief told me in no uncertain terms. 'Sir, neither do I know this boy nor have I ever seen him. How can I identify and trace him?' I asked him. 'You will be assisted by Inspector Syed, who knows the boy personally,' he assured me. Strangely, no photograph of the wanted boy was available. I was left with no choice but to comply. He gave me Ashraf's Bombay address as disclosed in the seized inland letter. 'You have to leave today,' he ordered. 'We have already blocked air seats for you and Inspector Syed.' I hurriedly packed my bag and departed for the airport where Syed was waiting. Syed, who had spent his entire career in the CID, was considered a major asset to the organization. Both of us boarded the plane and landed at Santa Cruz airport late in the evening. We checked into a sea-facing deluxe flat in Kashmir House in Colaba. The apartment was arranged by Dr Nishat, the J&K government's trade agent, who had been informed of our arrival by my boss.

The next morning, I called on the commissioner of Bombay Police for assistance and explained the whole issue to him. He detailed two senior CID inspectors to accompany us. Both of them asked for photographs of the wanted person but we had none. I felt very awkward whenever someone asked us to show the photograph of the wanted individual. It sounded very strange and unprofessional because we were dependent only on personal identification by the inspector accompanying me. Nevertheless, we had to carry on 'Mission Spy Chase' despite the absence of a photograph. With the help of CID sleuths, we located the residence of the Kashmiri business family with whom Ashraf was supposedly staying. We could not outrightly search the place as it was difficult in a location like Bombay. The Bombay Police also helped us locate the family's showroom on Link Road, behind the heritage Hotel Taj Mahal Palace, where many Kashmiri businessmen dealing in carpets and various Kashmiri handicrafts had their showrooms.

On my request, the Bombay CID kept a watch outside the suspected house with their men disguised as street vendors selling fruit on the pavement. They were briefed by Inspector Syed on Ashraf's physical appearance and other features. Similar arrangements were made in the street behind the Hotel Taj. Simultaneously, I decided to screen all mail addressed to the concerned business house, their employees or our wanted suspect. On my request, the police commissioner, who was empowered to permit pre-delivery censorship of mail in the interest of public order and security of the state, ordered the censoring of the requisite mail. Accordingly, the postmaster of the head post office was ordered to preserve the mail intended for our addressees and release it for delivery only after it was scrutinized by us. Sadly, no helpful information was found through this channel.

With no useful clue for many days, I decided to personally monitor the suspected business premises and occupied a vantage point on the spiral service stair of the hotel after getting the management on board. All day long, I watched the suspected showroom and the movement of the salesmen and customers without being noticed. However, there was no trace of Ashraf or any lookalike. Suddenly, after about more than a week, we came across a letter purportedly written by Ashraf to an employee of the business house already on our radar. The contents of the letter indicated that Ashraf had left for Delhi. He expressed his regret at being unable to formally say goodbye to them and his other friends before leaving. With this letter, we would have normally wound up our operations in Bombay. However, I guessed that Ashraf had probably come to know about our presence and activities in Bombay and had written the letter to mislead us so that we would roll back our surveillance. The other contents of the letter were irrelevant, but I somehow guessed that he was still in Bombay and keeping a close eye on our activities, including the censoring of his mail. It was truly a challenging battle of wits! Therefore, I decided to review our strategy and bring some changes in our covert and overt operations to give him the shock of his life. I decided to explore an additional but unexpected channel to track him down, without halting existing operations. Not taking anyone into confidence, and with only a faint idea of how to approach it, I thought of exploring the underworld.

Back in 1963–64, at a marriage party in Srinagar, my attention was caught by the presence of a tall ebony-skinned person with henna-dyed hair whom I had never seen before in the city. He received special attention from not only the host but also the other family members. Out of curiosity, I asked the host who the gentleman was. Without replying, he escorted me to his guest and introduced us to each other. He was Karim Khan, aka Karim Lala, a Bombay-based businessman whom I had heard of before. I spoke with him for a while. Apparently pleased to meet me, he extended a routine invitation to visit him in Bombay and stay with him. I did not take him very seriously and left after having my meal. My later inquiries revealed that he was a famous underworld don of Bombay.

Facing a setback in our operations, I thought of this man. 'Could he help?' I wondered. There was no harm in visiting him and exploring the possibility of enlisting his help. I called the Srinagar businessman who had introduced him to me, asked for Karim Khan's address and requested him to inform Karim Khan about my possible visit. Everything tied up to become what I named 'Mission Black Alleys'. It was like groping in the underworld without any prior experience. 'Mission Black Alleys' could backfire and cost me my career or even my life. With all the possible hazards ahead, I decided to take a leap into the underworld ocean without reckoning its depth, thinking such risks were part of the game I was supposed to play. I had no other option left as we were facing a sort of a dead end. I was determined to trace and pin down our wanted suspect in this overcrowded concrete jungle. It was like trying to find a needle in a haystack. Without informing Syed, I took a cab and asked the driver to drop me off in Dongri—the location provided by my Srinagar contact.

Accordingly, I embarked on a search for Karim Lala in Dongri, a vast locality of poverty-ridden people. When asked about his location, the shopkeepers of Dongri got up and readily offered to accompany me, which I politely refused. It didn't take me much time to realize his mighty clout in the area. Despite my polite refusal, one of the shopkeepers, in his overenthusiasm, voluntarily accompanied me to Café Rahimya, where Karim

Khan was supposed to be. At the café, I was told that he would not be available before evening. As it was afternoon, I decided to pass the time by watching a movie in a nearby theatre. In the evening, I returned to the café and someone pointed out the awe-inspiring tall, middle-aged man with henna-dyed hair sitting alone on an ordinary rope-string charpoy. He was feeding some goats in a narrow roadside in front of the café. Though I recognized him, I was apprehensive of his possible negative reaction, so I approached him cautiously and offered my salaam. Recognizing me, he got up and hugged me. He offered all the courtesies expected of a Pathan and behaved as if we had known each other for ages. Karim made me comfortable on the same charpoy and informed me about the phone call from our Srinagar contact who had briefed him about me. He asked for tea and in his Pathan dialect, asked me, 'What brings you to Bombay? When did you come?' 'I came here a few days ago on some official business,' I replied without showing any excitement.

The conversation went on, but I was very cautious with my words and confined myself to replying to his questions without being too inquisitive. He wanted to know about the tourist season in Kashmir and other such things. Tea was served. I wanted to take time before broaching the subject with him. While sitting together, I observed that almost every passer-by would say respectful salaams to him irrespective of their caste, creed, colour, age, sex and religious belief. After offering their salaam, most would not move ahead but stand silently a few yards away. Karim would take out some money from his pocket and give it to the man or woman standing in front of him. I also observed that the amount would vary from person to person. I could not resist and asked him, 'Who are these people, and why do you discriminate when you help them?' Smiling, he said, 'I know each one of them very well, and I also know their daily financial requirement.

Accordingly, I help them to the extent of their needs.' I silently appreciated this aspect of his life. To make it only a courtesy call, I asked for his leave. I thought I would come the next day and let him know my real purpose. He insisted that I should have dinner with him the following evening. I readily accepted his invitation to grab another opportunity to speak to him in a more congenial atmosphere.

The next evening, I returned alone to Café Rahimya. Sitting on the same charpoy, Karim was feeding the goats. I took my seat next to him on the charpoy, and after some time, unable to resist, I told him, 'I need some help from you but I don't know whether I should bother you with my problem. I have come here to arrest a young Kashmiri man who has been evading arrest for a long time.' To satisfy his curiosity about the crimes committed by the wanted man, he asked me many questions. He even wanted to know whether the wanted man was involved in any political game. I withheld some details for fear of his refusal to help in the arrest of an underground activist. To motivate him, I told him that the wanted man's arrest was a prestige issue for me and would enhance my respect in the eyes of my superiors. I made out a good case for a personal favour. When he asked me if I had a photograph of the wanted man, I felt embarrassed by the clumsiness of my department and told him, 'No, I don't have it, but I have an officer with me who can identify him.' He asked me to bring the officer along the next evening.

He then got up, and we got into his chauffeur-driven car and arrived at a place that did not seem to be his residence but a well-furnished hall in a flat that was spruced up for a musical evening. He had also invited a few of his friends; one of them was introduced to me as Haji Mastan Mirza, another chip off the same block about whom I had read a lot in the newspapers. He was a well-known underworld don of Bombay who later joined politics. After some Urdu ghazals were presented by a middle-aged robust woman, Naseem Bano, a sumptuous Afghan dinner was served, which I relished for its unique texture, taste and aroma.

Now, it was time to bring Syed into confidence. Returning from the dinner, I asked him to accompany me the next evening without sharing any details. The next day, both of us met Karim Khan at Café Rahimya, who was sitting on the same charpoy, tending to his goats. I introduced Syed to him. Karim Khan called two young Pathan men who were sitting away from him on a bench in front of the café. He asked me to brief them about the description, physical appearance, etc. of the wanted man. Syed, who was the only person who could do so, thoroughly briefed them about our wanted spy, including his possible hideouts in Bombay. On Karim's instructions, Syed also gave them the telephone number of the Kashmir Guest House in Bombay. I told Karim that I was leaving for Delhi the next morning and that Syed might contact him if required. Karim got up, hugged me and bid me an affectionate farewell. This was my last interaction with the top don of Bombay.

I flew to Delhi the next day after instructing Syed to not go anywhere and attend to the telephone 24×7. Putting my game plan into action, I left Bombay to give Ashraf the impression that his letter had had the desired effect and that we had rolled back our operations. This move also implied our mission's failure. I was sure that our fresh game plan would bring him out of hiding. I stayed in New Delhi for a few days and visited the hotels and residential areas where the Kashmiri business community, particularly those with whom Ashraf was staying in Bombay, lived. As a matter of abundant caution, I kept watch on a few places with the help of our New Delhi staff. I did not want to take the slightest chance in case the contents of his letter, censored in Bombay about his so-called departure, were true. Thereafter, I flew to Srinagar and briefed the CID chief. I then resumed my duties with the Ayyangar Commission.

After a few days, Syed informed me about Ashraf's arrest. The two Pathan trackers detailed by Karim Khan had phoned him about Ashraf's location in an ordinary Bombay hotel. Syed, along with the two Bombay CID officers assigned to us, reached the hotel and checked the register, but Ashraf's name was missing. The room that the Pathans had pinpointed was locked. The lock was opened by the manager with the help of a master key. A thorough search of the suitcase in the room produced a negative of a photograph, which was instantaneously processed and found to be Ashraf's picture. Bombay CID, assisted by Syed, laid a trap in and around the hotel. As soon as Ashraf came and unlocked his room, he was arrested. It was a clean but tedious operation courtesy of the underworld don Karim Lala. 'Mission Black Alleys' was wrapped up.

The next morning, Ashraf was flown to Srinagar but I had no occasion to meet him. My colleagues who questioned him told me that he admitted to posting the letter from Delhi to mislead us so that we would wind up and leave Bombay. Ashraf also disclosed that before our departure from Srinagar, he had been alerted by his associates as soon as we took the flight to Bombay. Subsequently, I learnt that his close confidant and associate, Bashir Ahmed Kichloo, who was also working for the PHC and had taken asylum there, had left for Delhi on the same plane which brought Ashraf to Srinagar. Both had exchanged optical greetings with each other. Bashir Kichloo is well-settled in London. He was reportedly smuggled out of India with the help of the PHC in New Delhi. One of his friends told me that over the years, he has visited Kashmir a couple of times with his family.

Thanks to CM Sadiq's liberalization policy, after his release from jail, Ashraf was appointed as an officer in the tourism department by the CM. Ashraf's uncle, Ghulam Ahmed, was Sadiq's private secretary. Specializing in adventure tourism, he ultimately retired as the Director General of Tourism.[6]

MIGRANTS REHABILITATED

In November 1967, I was posted to head the internal security section of the home department in the state secretariat to coordinate and facilitate the return and rehabilitation of families who had crossed the CFL into PoK in the wake of the 1965 war. In coordination with the district administration and other agencies, hundreds of families who returned with their livestock were rehabilitated back to their homes in the Poonch and Rajouri areas. The screening committee was headed by the deputy commissioner (DC) with the district SPs—CI division and special branch (SB), and local IB officers as members. CM G.M. Sadiq did not approve of the army's participation in such meetings despite their written request. He informed them that in a democratic set-up, the army had no role in civil matters. However, he advised them to convey their views or information, if any, to the DC concerned about any individual or group of individuals. It is believed that Sadiq got clearance from Prime Minister Indira Gandhi on the issue, although she was initially reluctant.[7] Sadiq had reportedly argued that if Indian citizens crossed over into enemy territory from any

---

[6]Some of the inputs in this story are from Ashraf himself. I interviewed him telephonically during the COVID-19 lockdown of 2020, only a few months before his death on 13 October.

[7]Kak, M.L., '50 Ultras Rearrested, J&K Bows under Centre's Pressure', *The Tribune*, 29 November 2002, https://m.tribuneindia.com/2002/20021129/. Accessed on 7 February 2024.

part of the country to save their lives during a war, they could they not be denied their right to return to their home after hostilities had ceased.

The Simla Agreement, signed by Indira Gandhi and Zulfiqar Ali Bhutto after the 1971 war, stipulated the conversion of the CFL into the LoC between India and Azad Kashmir (PoK). Initially, the army commanders of both countries cooperated with each other to demarcate the line along natural features like rivers, nallahs, hillocks and gallis. However, after the return of the prisoners of war (POWs), Pakistan adopted a rigid policy. They reportedly hardened their attitude regarding the demarcation of the LoC, leading to its demarcation along geographically unnatural features in most places. Consequently, many villages and families living near the newly marked LoC were placed in a disadvantageous position, thereby causing them a lot of suffering. One such instance was that of village Bara (Baade) in the Uri sector of Baramulla district in 1972.

WATERMILL RENDEZVOUS

After the 1965 war, Bara was divided into two unnatural parts, causing a lot of inconvenience and harassment to the residents. The Pakistani part of the village came to be known as Azad Bara, and the part on the Indian side was known as Bara. However, after the 1971 war, the LoC was redrawn and the whole village fell within the Indian territory. The LoC cut across a narrow hill stream, which could be crossed simply by jumping over to the other side. A watermill owned by a local of Bara existed downstream on the Indian side, where the residents of Bara and adjacent villages would get their grains ground. Intelligence agencies suspected the watermill to be a rendezvous point for Pakistani security personnel and their secret agents working on our side. It was also suspected that the villagers of Azad Bara were bringing grains for grinding at this watermill to interact with their neighbours. However, nothing substantial was ever established. The district police was never brought on board to sort out the issue. Surprise checks of the watermill were carried out several times by the army and other agencies but without any results.

One morning, I got a phone call from the SHO of a police station in Uri who informed me that an overzealous junior officer of one of the intelligence agencies had set the watermill on fire during the night, reducing it to ashes. The villagers of Bara and other neighbouring villages were very angry and agitated. Army sources also confirmed the incident; subsequently, I was able to identify the erring officer. I thought that this was the height of lawlessness and that too by a member of a disciplined organization. Had I ignored the issue, such incidents would have been repeated without consequences, leading to chaos in the border areas. The incident created a sense of fear in the minds of the entire border population. They feared that such unrestrained officials may even target civilian residences. Therefore, as a deterrent to such unlawful activities and to prevent such anti-people actions in the future, I immediately ordered the registration of an FIR for arson against the officer. The mere registration of the case had an immediate calming effect on the common people.

Meanwhile, I was contacted by the top brass of the agency whose officer was responsible for the arson. They tried to justify this unlawful act by arguing that the officer had done it in 'national interest' and that he had no personal axe to grind. I countered by saying that the constitution and the law of the land do not permit any such unlawful actions, even in 'national interest'. I argued that the officer had committed an anti-national act and nobody was above the law in this country, not even someone who committed a crime in 'national interest'. Additionally, I explained that this unlawful act was likely to alienate the border population who were otherwise helpful and usually cooperated with the armed forces. I frankly told them that I had no other option but to register the case. I also told the top brass of the organization that their officer should have approached the civil administration to shift the watermill, rather than taking the law into his own hands. I insisted that the erring officer be handed over to the police along with his accomplices. Several meetings were held between me and the agency officers.

Ultimately, a meeting was arranged at the higher level and after discussing the matter, I suggested a solution. I told them that the matter could only be dropped if the concerned agency offered to rebuild the gutted watermill at a different site, a few yards downstream, where there would be no possibility of Pakistani agencies misusing it as their rendezvous point. This was agreed to, and a new watermill was built downstream at a safe site, the cost of which was borne by the concerned agency. In this manner, the civil administration was able to uphold the law of the land with the cooperation of the senior officers of the concerned agency, as well as the army, who were also convinced that such unlawful acts by their officers were likely to alienate an otherwise cooperative local population. This action generated goodwill among the locals for not only the civil administration but also the security agencies, particularly the army at the LoC.

Shortly thereafter, another humanitarian problem erupted. The entire population of Bara, consisting of about 50 families, who had strayed into PoK in the wake of the 1971 war now wanted to return. Assembled across the LoC and clearly visible from our side, they even staged demonstrations against the Pakistani army who allegedly were preventing them from crossing back to resettle in Bara. I took up the matter personally with Major General S.C. Sinha, General Officer Commanding (GOC) 19 Infantry Division. After a couple of meetings with me and his other officers, it was decided to allow our migrant population to return and resettle in Bara after undergoing screening by all the concerned agencies.

Accompanied by a senior army officer from the area, I visited Bara to assess if the Pakistani army would cooperate. The situation remained unchanged. The migrant population raised slogans when they noticed us, demanding permission to return. Suddenly, the Baloch regiment guarding the LoC on the opposite side opened fire at us. Instantly, we took cover behind a big rock. I cautioned the officer accompanying me against retaliation, as it would likely harm the migrant villagers on the other side. We returned after taking the army officer into confidence about my next plan to bring back our migrants during the night. I am unable to share the plan in this book for ethical and security reasons. That same night, our migrants safely crossed over to our side along with their livestock. They were escorted by the army to Gohalan village near the highway because all of Bara had been mined during the war.

I informed my colleague, D.C. Hamidullah Khan, under whose orders the district administration made arrangements for tents, rations, medical aid, etc. at Gohalan. They were later allowed to resettle in Bara after the area was demined. Their plight after the onset of militancy and frequent firing along the LoC is unknown.

SPYING AND SMUGGLING

In the shadowy world of cloak and dagger, smuggling and spying are complementary; one cannot survive without the other. Sometimes, even spy handlers get involved in the lucrative world of smuggling. In 1973, while I was in my office in Baramulla, my office orderly brought in a slip of paper bearing the name of Colonel Bramhanand, who wanted to see me. I had never met this officer before but I had heard a lot about his activities as he looked after the army's intelligence wing. Due to his soft and affable manner, he had developed cordial relations with civilians throughout his area of responsibility. For reasons unknown to me, he had become a sort of household name in the villages along the LoC. Guessing the colonel had something important to convey, I had him ushered in.

A bulky middle-aged person in civvies and a karakul/astrakhan cap, commonly worn by the political leaders and influential persons of the Valley, entered, and I gestured him to take a chair. I asked for tea and instructed my orderly not to allow anyone to disturb us. As soon as the door closed, the colonel suddenly got up, took off his cap and dropped it at my feet. 'Sir, please save me. My honour and career are in your hands,' he begged of me. Shocked and embarrassed that a high-ranking and elderly army officer was touching my feet, I lifted him up, put his cap back on his head and made him comfortable in his chair. He was nearly in tears. I asked him to relax and tell me what the matter was. Colonel Brahmanand relaxed after I assured him of all possible help. Meanwhile, tea was served.

While narrating the story, the colonel told me that he was looking after the intelligence wing of the army in the entire Baramulla district, particularly along the LoC. 'Recently, some BSF personnel guarding the LoC in Tangdar area arrested a couple of infiltrators and deemed them to be my assets. The infiltrators were carrying a large consignment of astrakhan (karakul skin),' he said. He continued, 'Because of professional rivalry, the BSF officers were hell-bent on involving me personally in the smuggling of astrakhan, even though the infiltrating youth were strangers to me. Sir, I am innocent and not connected with the smuggling in any way. I don't even know the arrested persons who have been handed over to the local police by the BSF along with the smuggled consignment.'

The colonel believed that the BSF officers were trying to falsely implicate him by coercing the arrested persons into naming him as an accomplice. While I was patiently listening to him, he said, 'Sir, as you are visiting Tangdar tomorrow, I request you to please look into the matter personally so that I am not falsely implicated. My honour is in your hands.' I was not surprised at the colonel having advance information about my scheduled visit because the army was always informed about my movements in forward areas so that they could take proper precautions and make the necessary security arrangements at the place where I was staying for the night. I assured him that he had nothing to be worried about as the truth would prevail and he would surely not be falsely implicated in the case. He thanked me profusely and left my office highly satisfied.

I left for Tangdar the next morning. Surprisingly, the army was extraordinarily courteous all along the route, from Kupwara onwards, compared to my earlier visits. They had made elaborate arrangements for my rest and refreshments at different places en route. On reaching Tangdar, I checked in at the local dak bungalow where a major received me and led me to the VIP room reserved for me. The army telephone had already been installed as per practice. After freshening up, I started meeting the local people who had come in deputations from various areas to present their problems. This was my practice whenever I visited such far-flung border areas. Immediately thereafter, the same major returned with an invitation card from the brigade commander inviting me to dinner in the officers' mess that evening, which was as per protocol. During the day, I collected all the details about the colonel's alleged involvement in karakul/astrakhan smuggling. The SHO briefed me about the whole affair and its background. According to him, the infiltrators did not reveal any involvement of Colonel Brahmanand. I instructed the SHO to impartially and thoroughly investigate the matter so that nobody could question our findings later.

In the evening, I attended the dinner hosted by the brigade commander. Some local civilian officers had also been invited. The brigadier very casually touched upon the topic of karakul/astrakhan smuggling as I was leaving and requested me to look into the matter personally so that none of his officers would be unnecessarily dragged into the controversy. After assuring him of an unbiased and impartial investigation, I left.

The next day, the SHO was ready with a complete chargesheet that established that the smuggling of karakul skin was the exclusive venture of the infiltrators. The SHO told me that the sources engaged by various agencies to collect intelligence from across the LoC were generally making a few extra bucks by smuggling contraband goods as their normal remuneration was minimal. Incidentally, the local judicial magistrate had called on me in the morning. I requested him to take up the case for hearing on priority as the accused persons were likely to plead guilty. Accordingly, I instructed the SHO to produce the chargesheet the same day before the court so that the controversy could end in my presence once and for all. He produced the chargesheet in the court where the accused persons pleaded guilty. They did not name any other accomplice before the court, especially Colonel Brahmanand. They were sentenced to a few months of imprisonment. The confiscated karakul skin was ordered to be handed over to central customs authorities for further action under the law. The police secured the conviction of the accused only for their unlawful infiltration across the LoC and not for smuggling, as that was beyond their legal jurisdiction. The police had no powers under the Customs Act. Taking further action under the law was left to the customs authorities. In this manner, the self-respect and honour of our elderly officer, Colonel Brahmanand, was preserved.

Smuggling activities are common across the LoC and India's international border. The smuggling is patronized and carried out by interested agencies/groups/persons with the help of some unscrupulous elements. However, such activities are not possible without the connivance of the forces guarding the LoC on both sides. Drones are also used for dropping drugs and weapons. The free availability of lethal drugs jeopardizes the health and safety of the people, particularly the youth. Since the onset of militancy, J&K state has become a significant route within the Golden Crescent for smuggling charas, heroin, weapons, etc. In the hinterland of the Valley, poppy and bung cultivation is carried out on thousands of acres of cultivable land, particularly in the Kulgam, Shopian and Pulwama districts of south Kashmir. So far, this problem has not been very seriously dealt with either by the state or central agencies, who are only interested in chance seizures and do not rope in cultivators or the mafia who purchase the standing crops in advance. Officers of various law enforcement agencies are suspected of abetting this unlawful cultivation. Moreover, J&K Police allege that drug smuggling is the latest source of terror funding.

INTELLIGENCE GATHERING

I never had any position in the administration or an assignment or mandate to operate any agents on the other side of the LoC or the international border. Whatever information I obtained about happenings on the other side was gathered from arrested spies, agents or infiltrators, either launched by some agency or genuine visitors to their separated families. The actual sources of my information were the common people of border areas who were always welcome in my office and residence with their grievances. I would sit for hours with them to inquire, not only about the happenings in their area but also the other side. Whatever information I got was sufficient for my administrative requirements. Had I been posted in the Kashmir Range in 1987 and early 1988, I may not have missed the Inter-Services Intelligence's (ISI) grand plan of recruiting the Kashmiri youth for arms training and their crossing the LoC into PoK. Nevertheless, destiny took its own course.

HONEYTRAP

I am tempted to share the story of Captain Rashid, an important ISI asset. Although not an army officer, he was nicknamed 'Captain' by his handlers. Hailing from a border village in north Kashmir on the Indian side, Captain Rashid permanently migrated to PoK after he allegedly double-crossed some Indian agency. In early 1988, the ISI used his services as a guide for the Kashmiri youth crossing the LoC for arms and training; he was also tasked with sabotage, subversion and assassination within the Valley. Rashid was, therefore, a frequent visitor to the Valley. In this process, he established a hideout with a family in the hinterlands of north Kashmir, not very far from the LoC. The local police had acquired highly sensitive information that Rashid had allegedly established an intimate relationship with a female member of the family. Our officers in the concerned police station managed to take the female into confidence, and she promised to cooperate. Rashid's next visit to meet his love proved to be his last. He was trapped by our offficers and arrested, despite being armed.

As soon as I got the information, I immediately passed it on to CM Farooq Abdullah, who was touring Sopore. With a view to project the meritorious job done by my junior colleagues, I asked them to bring Rashid to the Sopore dak bungalow and also requested the CM and the Director General of Police (DGP) to drop by. Everything happened in such a hurry that the police could not even question him in detail about his activities.

Captain Rashid was a young man in his thirties. Before I could even talk to him, Dr Farooq arrived and was face to face with the prize catch. On my request, he announced a one-rank promotion for each member of the team involved in Rashid's arrest, which my boss, the DGP, resisted as he was a stickler for rules. I overcame his objections by arranging for a press note from the state information department about the CM's orders, thus closing all options for the DGP to block the process. Within a day or so, he issued the promotion orders. Captain Rashid was relaxed while sitting in front of the CM, whom he could not identify. As soon as we told him about the CM's identity, he was very happy and narrated a bone-chilling story.

Rashid stated that he had been a regular visitor to the Valley for the last few years, first as an ISI agent and later as a guide for militants. Continuing his statement, he said that in 1988, the ISI assigned him the task of assassinating Dr Farooq Abdullah. To execute the plan, he had selected a spot in Srinagar—Gulmarg Road—to target Farooq when he was informed about his scheduled visit to Gulmarg. He had taken his position in a strategically suitable spot on the roadside well before the arrival of the CM's motorcade. While waiting there, his local collaborator, who was with him to identify Dr Farooq, casually mentioned to Rashid that Dr Farooq's mother belonged to the Gujjar tribe of

Tangmarg. Addressing Dr Farooq, he said, 'Once I heard that, I instantly abandoned the plan to assassinate you as I was also a Gujjar. I deliberated why I should kill one of my Gujjar bhais.' The CM's face went pale but he listened to the whole story with a smile. God has his own ways to save a person's life, I thought. Later, Captain Rashid escaped from Srinagar Central Jail in an allegedly manipulated jailbreak. He didn't live long thereafter. He was reportedly killed by an important Hizb-ul-Mujahideen commander who suspected Rashid of intimacy with his wife. Even his dead body could not be found.

Two more secret agents and saboteurs, Nizam-ud-Deen, aka Babar, and Sadiq, were active in 1988 and 1989. Babar was initially responsible for motivating Ghulam Nabi Bhat, the brother of Maqbool Bhat, and Abdul Ahad Waza (a People's Conference activist) to visit PoK, where the plan to initiate armed revolt was disclosed to them by some Pakistani army officers as well as Amanullah Khan and his colleagues. They were tasked with recruiting youth and sending them to PoK for arms and training. Back in the Valley, they also got the nod for the same from their leader, Abdul Ghani Lone.

THE COLLABORATORS

During the infiltration by the Pakistani Mujahideen in 1965, the majority of the population of J&K was indifferent towards them for want of any sufficient information regarding local pro Pakistan or pro-plebiscite leadership. However, numerous youngsters and a section of the PF led by one Haji Ishaq provided logistic and other support to them, thus leaving behind some interesting stories. It is believed that the fleeing Mujahideen dumped arms, ammunition and military hardware at some unknown places, which could not be retrieved by the police, army or intelligence agencies.

In 1965, after the India-Pakistan war, a CI officer, who was my colleague and good friend, called me and requested a meeting. The following day, he arrived at my residence and we discussed the matter over a cup of tea. He told me that a suspect in his custody at the JIC was not cooperating; he was believed to have cached a large number of arms and explosives left behind by the Mujahideen at some secret location. The suspect, according to him, was a tough nut to crack. 'Now, the difficulty is that he is behaving as if he has lost all his mental faculties and gone insane. I want your help,' he told me. 'How can I help? You should get him examined by a psychiatrist,' I replied. 'No, you can help. You know him very well, and I want you to meet him once to persuade him to cooperate.' I found it amusing that I was being asked to persuade a prisoner to confess. He continued, 'The suspect is Ahmad Shah Bazaz, a resident of Khanqah-e-Moula and a distant relative of yours. It will be a huge favour if you speak to him and find out if he is really insane.' I refused, saying that it would be unethical to quiz someone outside the domain of my duty. Nevertheless, on his insistence, I agreed to meet Ahmad Shah Bazaz in my personal capacity only to ask about his welfare and nothing else. The officer agreed.

Ahmad Shah Bazaz was a well-known freedom fighter who had served several jail terms and even received a sentence of whipping during the freedom movement against the Maharaja's rule. Later, he was awarded the Tamra Patra. After the dismissal and arrest of Sheikh Mohammad Abdullah on 9 August 1953, Bazaz was repeatedly arrested and confined as a dedicated worker of the PF. Now, the interrogators, including my friend, had failed to break him or secure his confession regarding the recovery of arms.

Ahmad Shah Bazaz was known to me as a distant relation and

neighbour right from my early childhood. He was my phupha's (my aunt's husband) brother. A typical middle-aged Kashmiri, he was a dedicated and blind follower of Sheikh Mohammad Abdullah. Not being a man of substance, he married very late in his life. Bazaz had two sons and two daughters, who were very young when he went to jail. To make ends meet, he dealt in second-hand auctioned goods and had a humble sales outlet in Dukaan-e-Sangeen, a locality near his home in downtown Srinagar. He had a sort of weakness for me and loved me like his own son but never divulged any information to me about his covert activities. I never bothered him about it as I thought it unprofessional and unethical to take advantage of my personal relations and ask for information that I was not officially authorized to know.

As a party, the PF remained indifferent to the Pakistani Mujahideen as they had not been brought on board in advance. However, a senior PF leader and prominent transporter, Haji Mohammad Ishaq, was enthusiastic to render help to the retreating Mujahideen. He roped in some other prominent workers of the PF, including Bazaz. They provided logistical assistance and hideouts to individual Mujahideen members within the Valley and allegedly cached their arms, ammunition and explosives. This was in utter violation of the policy of non-interference adopted by the PF leadership, who were incarcerated in different jails. The Ishaq group, nicknamed Kharji Mahazi (ousted Mahazis), was later expelled from the PF. Sheikh Mohammad Abdullah was reportedly very angry with this breach of discipline. With this background, Ahmad Shah Bazaz was allegedly an active collaborator of the Mujahideen as a member of the Ishaq group and knew about arms caches.

My colleague facilitated my meeting with Bazaz at JIC Srinagar, where he was confined in a small separate room. As soon as I entered his room and was within his hearing range, I said my salaam, as is customary, 'Assalaam u Alaikum.' However, Bazaz neither reacted nor appeared to have noticed my presence. He did not even look towards me. He was talking to himself incoherently in a soft voice but his general appearance did not give any indication of insanity. My continued efforts to draw his attention towards me failed. Throughout the interview, he behaved as if he was alone in the room. Even after staying with him for quite some time and trying to draw him into a conversation, I could not get any response. Therefore, I left after saying my salaam, once again with no response from him. I could not draw any conclusion one way or the other, though I suspected that the prolonged solitary confinement might have affected his mental state. I told my CI friend exactly what I felt.

After some time, Bazaz was reportedly transferred to Srinagar Central Jail as the CI officers failed to get any useful information from him. His wife, who would often go to see him, believed his insanity to be genuine. One of his jail mates, Mohammad Youssef Bhat, recorded in his book, 'He (Bazaz) usually sits near the gates, and whoever goes out, he suspects them of having given false testimony (sic) against him.' Pointing to his fellow detenus, he used to say, 'There he goes to give false testimony (sic) against me. This is a shocking experience. He has been rendered schizophrenic.'[8]

As soon as I was informed about his release after a long spell of detention, I was very curious to see him. As I entered his room, he got up and hugged me affectionately. He told me he knew that I had been sent to the JIC to meet him just to confirm whether he was really insane. With his tall figure looming large

[8]Bhat, Mohammad Youssef, *Prison Diary—Kashmir Untold Story, 1965–68*, Mohammad Youssef Bhat, Srinagar, 2017, 63.

in the room, I wondered how had he feigned insanity for several years in detention. To my knowledge, he was the only person who did not disclose any self-incriminating material in the JIC. Bazaz died on 30 January 1984, carrying all the secrets of his covert life to his grave, including the location of the suspected cache of arms. He succeeded in concealing everything he knew about the shadowy world of covert warfare.

After the Indira–Sheikh Accord of 1975, the lower rung of Kharji Mahazis, including Ahmad Shah Bazaz but excluding Haji Ishaq, again came within the fold of Sheikh's National Conference. Ahmad Shah Bazaz would often visit Sheikh with humble gifts, such as a bundle of lotus roots (nadru) or a delicacy of Kashmiri vegetarian cuisine. However, he did not get any favours from the state for his children. His elder son, Showkat, was initially appointed as a class IV employee in the health department but was removed from service for being publicly rude to an NC leader. Later, Showkat followed in his father's footsteps in terms of vocation and is doing well. Shah's two daughters completed their master's but could not get a job. Nevertheless, both were lucky to find good life partners and are well-settled with a happy family.

Unfortunately, his second son, Aijaz, joined militancy in 1990 and was the commander of Al Jehad. His mother was very concerned about his safety and would often come to me for advice, even after my retirement. I always advised her to convince her son about her concerns rather than relying on my advice. However, Aijaz later crossed the LoC into PoK around 1994, never to return. He is said to have settled in Muzaffarabad after marrying a Kashmiri girl from Baramulla. He is reportedly engaged in some business venture there.

Another dedicated worker of the PF, Ghulam Nabi Peer, a resident of the rural district of Budgam, was a lorry agent who earned his livelihood by booking bus passengers for a meagre commission. In August 1965, as soon as he found out about the presence of Pakistani infiltrators in his district, he established contact with them and voluntarily assumed the role of their guide. With his collaboration and valuable guidance, the Mujahideen launched an attack on the Budgam Police Station and looted the whole armoury. Additionally, with his input and active assistance, the Pakistani infiltrators launched a surprise attack on an Indian army formation in the district, causing substantial loss of life. As the infiltrators retreated, Peer, fearing retaliation and death at the hands of the army, crossed the LoC into PoK with the retreating Mujahideen. He was believed to have knowledge of the cached arms. A couple of months later, he was back home. The following story is based on his confession before the special court.

No importance whatsoever was given to him either in PoK or in Pakistan by the Mujahideen, whom he had helped while retreating. While Peer had expected VIP treatment, the Pakistani army authorities showed no interest in providing him assistance to get rehabilitated or even a minor job. In Pakistan, he depended on a group of Kashmiri labourers at the Rawalpindi railway station for his two meals on the condition that he would be their cook. After facing a humiliating situation, someone advised him to see Hamidullah Khan, the then president of PoK, for a government job; he thought that a job would surely be provided to him in view of his assistance to the Mujahideen and track record as a staunch worker of the PF. With much difficulty, he secured an audience with the president in his office at Muzaffarabad. Tasbih in hand, the president asked him to come on the first of the next month so that he would be in a position to provide him some monetary assistance out of his own salary. This was an utter shock to Peer. He only pitied the helplessness of the poor president and left.

Finding no foothold there, Peer decided to return to the

Valley, which was not very easy. He thought of two possible difficulties: one, the Pakistani Army would not allow him to cross the CFL, and two, even if he succeeded, once in the Valley, he feared a grave threat to his life at the hands of the Indian Army. Though illiterate, Peer was very clever and intelligent. Therefore, he contacted the Pakistani Intelligence and offered them his services as a courier, spy or even a saboteur. Given his clean and favourable image, he was brought into their fold and given the task of arranging some bomb blasts in Srinagar. A Gujjar guide was provided to him with some live hand grenades and other supplies. Before entering the Indian side of the CFL, Peer established contact with the CI wing of the J&K police through an intermediary. With his help, Peer offered to surrender to them on the assurance that he would not be handed over to the army. The concerned head of the CI accepted the offer. All loose ends were tied up. On the stipulated date, Peer crossed the CFL undetected via Sawjian in Mandi in the Poonch area and surrendered to the CI staff somewhere in Beerwah, from where he was whisked away to JIC Srinagar.

Peer was thoroughly questioned by all agencies, including the army. The CI might have involved the army and assured them of stringent action against Peer. He openly confessed to all the agencies regarding his role as a collaborator of the Mujahideen. but claimed ignorance about any cached arms. The CI got his confession recorded under section 164 of the Code of Criminal Procedure (CrPC). After the investigation was completed, a chargesheet was produced before a special court in Srinagar Central Jail. I was appointed as the special public prosecutor to represent the state in the case.

On the day of the hearing, Ghulam Nabi Peer was produced before the special court at Srinagar Central Jail. The court was presided over by Sessions Judge Mohan Kishen Tickoo. Tickoo was also the presiding officer of the special court in the Kashmir Conspiracy Case against Sheikh Abdullah and other leaders in Kud and later in Jammu. Sheikh, much impressed by his impartial behaviour, appointed Tickoo as a government minister after the Indira–Sheikh Accord of 1975.

Exuding immense confidence, Ghulam Nabi Peer stood in the dock. The proceedings were short and crisp. No witnesses were required to be examined and no arguments were to be advanced; he openly confessed before the trial court and was sentenced to seven years' imprisonment.

After earning routine remissions in his sentence for his good behaviour as a prisoner, Peer was released after a short duration of imprisonment. Upon his release, he resettled in his native village and led a normal life. I don't know whether he is still alive.

SAUDI UNDERCOVER AGENT

In the early 1980s, a Saudi national, Abdul Ghani Malik, appeared on the scene in Srinagar. Malik had a keen interest in exporting Kashmiri handicrafts to Saudi Arabia. With the good offices of a professional photographer who was dependent on tourism for his livelihood, Malik was introduced to a cross-section of society in Srinagar, including businessmen, civil servants and politicians. Malik claimed to be of Kashmiri origin and related to Nawaz Sharif, the then prime minister of Pakistan. Though a Pakistani national, he claimed to be a naturalized Saudi citizen settled in the holy city of Makkah. He could converse with ease in Urdu, Punjabi and Arabic.

Malik visited Kashmir repeatedly for some years, ostensibly for business. He roped in the photographer and lured him into the trade of exporting carpets. Over time, he developed intimate relations with a prominent separatist politician and a couple of businessmen. At that time, I had no reason to suspect Malik's bona fide, and no state or central intelligence agency had conveyed any suspicion about him. In hindsight, I strongly believe Malik may have introduced Abdul Ghani Lone to the ISI, who was later preferred by Muhammad Zia-ul-Haq and the top brass of the ISI as their own asset to initiate an armed uprising of Kashmiri youth.

It is believed that the politician's son began exporting gold jewellery from India to Gulf countries for which he was allowed to draw solid gold from the Minerals & Metals Trading Corporation, GoI. Whether the Corporation recovered the value of the gold from him is unknown. A substantial quantity of gold jewellery is claimed to have been ultimately misappropriated by one of Malik's nephews, who is said to own a tin factory in Jeddah. Malik's photographer friend, who got into the carpet business through Malik and had a showroom in Jeddah, is believed to be bankrupt now, allegedly due to the actions of Malik's nephew.

In retrospect, I suspect that Malik may have successfully established a reasonably strong base for the ISI in the Valley, which may have been useful to them to initiate the militancy in 1988. Needless to say, his politician friend and family in the Valley were pioneers key figures of militancy initiated by Zia-ul-Haq.

DOUBLE AGENTS

In the early 1970s, a small-time trader dealing in smuggled goods, such as imported transistor sets, VCRs, cigarettes, perfumes, dinner sets, tea sets, men's and women's clothing, etc. appeared on the scene. His residence-cum-retail outlet was situated in a small lane in Naid Kadal in downtown Srinagar on the ground floor of his rickety ancestral house. The local police did not bother taking action against him because they didn't have any power under the Customs Act and because their hands were full with day-to-day resistance-related law and order problems. Customs authorities also ignored such small dealers because of their policy of not wasting their resources and time on petty traders. In those days, such smuggled items were openly sold by pavement vendors, even in Mumbai. Over time, the trader had faded from my memory.

In 2006, a friend wanted my advice on whether he should purchase a particular housing plot somewhere on the Srinagar bypass. Though I had no expertise on the subject, I accompanied him to the site for his satisfaction. I saw the plot and advised him to go for it as the area was likely to develop in due course of time.

After a few days, my friend approached me in a state of panic and informed me that the plot vendor had been arrested by the police before he could sign the sale deed, although he had received full payment. 'Who is the vendor? What is his name, and where does he live?' I asked him. 'His name is Ismail [name changed], and he is lodged at such and such place [location withheld].' I was shocked to learn that the vendor was the same petty smuggled goods dealer whom I knew by name but had never seen. I did not intervene and steered clear of my friend by advising him to wait for a few days. 'He may be released on bail or something.' After a few days, he came again and told me that Ismail had not been released. Left with no alternative, I rang up one of my former colleagues and inquired why the vendor had been arrested and if there were any chances of his early release. 'Ha Ha Ha,' he laughed heartily. 'Sir, it depends on his own sweet whim and fancy when to come into or go out of custody,' he said. I was confused. 'What do you mean? I don't understand,' I asked him. 'I am not his handler, but I only know he is detained with his own consent and will remain there as long as he likes. I can't share anything more,' he said. I was further confused because I had not come across such a character in my career. Frankly, what I could make out was that he must have been an important asset to the intelligence agencies and was in custody as part of some covert operation. A few days, later the vendor was released and he signed my friend's sale deed.

A few years later, Ismail's son Manzoor (name changed), who was engaged in the carpet business somewhere in the Gulf, was arrested in Delhi. It was officially stated that ₹55 lakh was seized from him by the Enforcement Directorate, along with some arms, explosives, etc. Nobody believed that any sane person would carry so much cash and illegal items on a regular international flight and directly land at the Indira Gandhi International Airport in Delhi. It is speculated that Manzoor might have been called by his Indian handler, who then pinned all this stuff on him to blackmail him into being part of a big game. It is not difficult to guess that the recovered cash and lethal stuff must have been planted on him. Otherwise, given his poor reputation as a hawala operator, he would not have risked flying to Delhi.

A lot of publicity was given to this successful covert operation. Knowledgeable sources told me that when some Hurriyat leaders met with Prime Minister Vajpayee and Home Minister L.K. Advani in New Delhi, one of them reportedly recommended Manzoor's release—the only point on his agenda. Subsequently, in 2008, Manzoor was granted bail on the condition that ₹35 lakh cash would be deposited in the court as surety. As soon as he was bailed out, he is claimed to have jumped bail, disappeared and safely landed abroad. Authorities say he escaped via Nepal but insiders believe he took a normal flight and was seen off by his Indian intelligence friends and handlers at the Indira Gandhi International Airport.

His father was a known hawala operator, who, over time, had risen to become a real estate dealer by investing a lot of hawala money to purchase land in the Valley. I believe that the father–son duo were double agents. The cash bail was naturally forfeited by the court. No attempt was made to extradite him, and his name never again appeared in the media. He is a forgotten figure now. Surprisingly, operators like Manzoor play for both sides. One wonders why Manzoor was not extradited when the GoI could capture Christian James Michel, the alleged middleman of the AugustaWestland VVIP Helicopter Scam from the Gulf. Manzoor may be a more important asset, despite the allegations of terror funding levelled against him.

It was learnt that when Manzoor's daughter was to be married in Srinagar in the autumn of 2019, the family booked two five-star hotels for different ceremonies. Manzoor must have attended the wedding with the help of his handlers in India.

Chapter 2

Three Aces

FIRST BANK ROBBERY

On 2 January 1971, while I was busy inspecting the Shergarhi Police Station in southern Srinagar, I received an alarming phone call from the police control room (PCR) about a daylight robbery at the Hazratbal branch of the Jammu & Kashmir Bank. A group of youngsters dressed in police uniforms had arrived in a taxi and allegedly looted the bank. This being the first bank robbery in the history of the state, an alert was sounded and checkpoints were established all over the city and its suburbs. All the entry and exit points in the Valley, including the Jawahar Tunnel on the national highway, were also secured. No more details were available.

Though the incident had not occurred in my subdivision, in view of the gravity of the crime, we acted swiftly by alerting all police stations and sending out multiple police parties across the city to locate the unidentified robbers and the Ambassador taxi used by them. After a couple of hours, the car was found abandoned at Kawadara, a downtown locality of Srinagar. The robbers had vanished. In the evening, all the senior officers and SHOs of the city were summoned for a meeting at the Kothibagh Police Station by DIG Peer Ghulam Hassan Shah to assess the situation. The bank manager, a Kashmiri Pandit gentleman, and his other staff members were also there for questioning.

The bank manager stated that he had drawn cash from the State Bank of India, Residency Road, Srinagar, that morning, to disburse salaries, especially to the Kashmir University staff. He had hardly commenced the disbursement when a group of uniformed 'police officers' arrived at the bank and informed him about suspected embezzlement at the State Bank of India and directed him not to make any disbursement. They asked him to put all the cash in a box and accompany them. Without hesitation or getting suspicious, the bank manager acted accordingly. No force was used and no weapons were displayed or used by any of the 'policemen'. After driving a few kilometres on Hazratbal–Lal Bazar Road, they stopped at an isolated place, pushed the manager out of the car and drove away. The shocked bank manager walked back to the bank and informed his staff about the incident. He lodged a report at the Nageen Police Division, situated only about 200 yards from the bank. The initial investigation was enough to show that the robbery had been committed with foolproof planning and precision, leaving no traces behind.

INITIAL BREAKTHROUGH

While questioning the bank staff that evening at the Kothibagh Police Station, a junior assistant named Mohammad Maqbool revealed that he recognized one of the individuals in uniform who, according to him, was probably his batchmate from SP College, Srinagar. However, he was surprised to see him in a police uniform because he knew the individual to be a science student and could hardly imagine him as a police officer. Maqbool knew neither his name nor residential address; he only knew that he was a villager and not a city dweller. Though this was a very weak and flimsy clue, the investigators had no choice but to pursue it. Therefore, the principal of SP College was contacted the same night, and all the admission forms of the relevant year bearing the candidates' photographs were brought to the police station. Maqbool was asked to closely examine the photographs. Despite being a time-consuming exercise, it proved fruitful. Around midnight, Maqbool was able to identify the suspect from the photograph of the admission form. The entries in the admission form revealed the young man to be Farooq Ahmed Bhat, a resident of Prang village in present-day Bandipore district. This discovery was shocking for all of us as Farooq's father, Abdul Khaliq Bhat, was a senior leader of the ruling party and a Member of the Legislative Assembly (MLA). Some quick inquiries revealed that Farooq was a student at Government Medical College, Srinagar, and had no previous criminal history. I recollected that during my days as a young police officer, when Farooq was still in school, he habitually stole cars and motorbikes parked on the roadside for joyrides and would abandon them after a trip in what were considered as schoolboy pranks. His father's residence in Saderkote Bala, near Bandipore, was searched the same night by a special police party, but Farooq was missing. No incriminating evidence was found from the house. Farooq's identification was the initial breakthrough and was sufficient for the investigators to continue the probe.

The next day, IGP Surendra Nath ordered the formation of a special team of selected officers headed by me to exclusively investigate the first bank robbery of the state, though the place of the occurrence did not fall under my jurisdiction. Because of the seriousness of this unprecedented and sensational crime, I was directed to operate from the JIC where the entire set-up, including the staff, was placed at my disposal. Elaborate arrangements for food, bedding, heating, etc. were made at the JIC for possible witnesses, suspects and others who were likely to be summoned. All the details of the case were discussed among this elite group of investigators who were broadly divided into two groups. One group was detailed to the field to try and locate Farooq's whereabouts and contact his relations and friends in Srinagar and other places to find any information that could lead us to him. The other group was responsible for questioning the suspects and scanning the documentation at the JIC. The collected information was evaluated, discussed and assessed every day, and follow-up action was taken as needed. Initially, we questioned Farooq's brothers and other known relations; with their help, a list of his classmates, friends and acquaintances was compiled. All of them were summoned and interrogated but no useful clue was found. Because this crime was the first of its kind, we could not think of any known criminal, as at the time, no one in the whole state had the modus operandi for looting a bank. Nevertheless, our determination and resolve made us move forward and continue our task undeterred. The morale of my staff was very high. It was a challenge to the entire police fraternity of the state and its top leadership, as none of us wanted the first bank robbery to go unsolved.

FRIEND OR DECOY

A few days after taking over the investigation, while on my way to the JIC, I regularly stopped at the famous Mir Pan House on Regal Chowk, Residency Road, to have paan (betel leaf). Abdul Raman Mir, the proprietor, whom I knew from my student days, was always well-informed about the daily happenings in the city. Our gossip would cover political developments, the state of crime in the city, rumours, love stories of boys and girls in nearby colleges, and so on. Though semi-literate, Mir was a good conversationalist with an affable manner and a wide range of contacts in all sections of society, including the police, civil servants, politicians, students, poets, writers, journalists, academics and artists. He was sort of an asset to me in my profession, but I never let him suspect that I was taking any professional advantage of him; otherwise, he would have hesitated to talk frankly.

I visited him deliberately to find out what the grapevine was saying about the bank robbery. As I stood in front of his shop after exchanging routine greetings, he offered me a paan. He asked me point blank, 'Is it true that you have been entrusted with the Hazratbal Bank Robbery Case?' I was taken aback, as it was an internal departmental arrangement and wasn't public knowledge. I wondered how he came to know about it. Without showing any excitement or questioning him about the source of his information, I replied in the affirmative. He told me, 'My son, Mohammad Yusuf, was a batchmate of the missing suspect, Farooq, at Biscoe School, and both were good friends.' I was shocked. How did he know about Farooq having been identified as the prime suspect? He continued, 'Yusuf can be of great help to you.' Though this was a welcome offer, I deliberately did not show much enthusiasm. 'Send him to my home whenever he likes,' I casually told him while leaving his shop.

The next morning, I found Yusuf in the drawing room of my Jawaharlal Nagar residence. I knew that he had been briefly arrested for stone pelting as a student during anti-India demonstrations at SP College the year before. I could not help but slightly suspect Yusuf's bona fides because of his voluntary offer to help, and that too without losing any time. I played it cool and did not deem it proper to talk to him at my home. As I was leaving for the JIC, I asked him to accompany me in the back of my jeep. At the JIC, I made him comfortable in my office chamber and called for tea. I did not hand him over for questioning to any of my staff as they would not have approached him as I had planned. We talked about lighter topics, such as movies, his daily activities, his career, his future plans, happenings in the city, students' demonstrations, etc. When asked what he knew about Farooq, our prime suspect, he gave me names of his batchmates and friends, which I already knew. By his general demeanour, he was a shrewd young man—introverted and careful in selecting his words while speaking. He seemed to be trying to withhold more than what he revealed, which strengthened my suspicion about him. With no worthwhile input from him and his continuously framed replies to my questions, I asked him a simple but unexpected question, which I thought would either clear or disprove his bona fides, 'Did you voluntarily tell your father that you could help me, or did your father suggest you help me in this investigation?' 'I told my father that I would be able to help Watali when I heard Farooq was the suspect.' My suspicion was strengthened. I thought that he knew much more and might have offered to 'help' me with two objects in mind: one, to mislead me in my investigation as far as possible, and two, to gather as much information as he could regarding the various lines of investigation pursued by us to possibly alert the actual culprits and their associates. He seemed to be part of a bigger game, I thought.

Now, I changed my soft tone of talking to him as the son of a friend. Instead, I firmly directed him to stand up and listen to me. He complied and meekly stood up. 'Listen, you are a plant, a decoy and not a friend,' I declared. He kept his head down and did not answer. He did not say anything to defend himself or dispel my suspicion. He was apparently shell-shocked. Despite my suspicions, I deferred my questioning till I was armed with further information. 'From now onwards you are my guest here. You will stay with me,' I declared. I advised him to try and recollect whatever he could about Farooq. I asked my staff to make him comfortable in a separate room and not to quiz him without my permission. I also instructed them to not allow any outsider to meet or talk to him.

MEDICAL COLLEGE HOSTEL ROOM

While investigations were ongoing, extra care was taken to maintain a low profile and utmost secrecy so that the media or public did not suspect any unusual activity on our part. We ensured that no information gathered by us or the arrest of any suspect leaked to jeopardize our investigations. Despite our efforts, our investigation was moving at a slow pace. By that time, only two facts were clear: one, Farooq was a student of Government Medical College, Srinagar, and two, he had been living in the college hostel at Bamina, where he had not been seen since the crime was committed. Although the hostel was closed for winter vacations, I decided to personally check his hostel room for any possible clue secretly, without even letting the medical college authorities in on the plan. I didn't want the perpetrators of the sensational crime to get alerted.

We had confirmed the location and number of his room from his relatives, friends and classmates during questioning. Only one chowkidar was present at the hostel whom we asked to accompany us without informing him of our real mission. Accompanied by another officer, I entered the hostel with the chowkidar following behind and broke open the lock of Farooq's room. It looked like a typical student's room, with books, notebooks and papers lying scattered. There were also some good colour paintings and pencil drawings. We picked up a couple of diaries, notebooks and a bunch of his girlfriend's love letters. Before leaving, we gave strict instructions to the chowkidar to keep his mouth shut. I handed over the collected stuff to one of my officers at the JIC for scrutiny with instructions to point out any suspicious. However, I was very disappointed, demoralized and discouraged when the officer, while placing the collected evidence on my table, told me that nothing useful was found. With this, I lost all hope and was unable to think of any other possible line of investigation. A sort of inertia hit me; I had hit a dead end, I thought. However, I instantly recovered from the shock and did not give up hope and self-confidence. I asked the officer to leave the material with me. I had no reason to doubt his professional competence and re-examine the material.

THE CRYPTIC NOTEBOOK

Feeling like I had nothing constructive to do, I casually picked up a tiny notebook from the pile and turned its pages to read the 'useless' writings. Gradually, my urge to continue the scrutiny grew in the hope of finding some clue. I read through each and every word of all the documents. While going through a pocket-sized notebook, my attention was caught by a list of seven names with a code consisting of five to six numbers and two letters at the end of each. Each number and letter was different from the other. I tried my best to concentrate and guess the identities but could not, as the names and surnames were so common that one could not decipher anything. Though one name was Mohammad Yusuf Mir, I decided not to confront Yusuf at that stage, fearing that he might mislead me. I avoided taking that risk. Though I knew a young resident of Verinag with the same name who was engaged in anti-India activities, I deferred summoning him. He was the leader of a student and youth outfit.

The numbers, I guessed, could be codes of the persons whose names were recorded therein. Moreover, a medical college student had no business making such cryptic notes. To clarify my doubts,

I called the officer who had already scrutinized the documents and inquired from him if he had seen the page or tried to decipher the unusual numbers. 'Sir, these are lottery ticket numbers,' he declared confidently. Though I had seen lottery tickets, I had no personal interest in the game. Purchasing lottery tickets was a common craze among the poor and middle class, particularly the youth. Doubting the officer's opinion, I told him, 'I think serial numbers on a lottery ticket start with one letter. In the notebook, there are two letters at the end of the number, so these cannot be lottery ticket numbers.' He did not react to my observation. To confirm or rule out whether these were lottery ticket numbers, I called Muzafer, the SHO of the Maisuma Police Station, asking him to check the lottery tickets of all the states on sale in the market. 'Collect the serial numbers printed on the tickets of each state and pass them on to me immediately,' I directed him. Soon after, he called back and dictated the serial numbers of the tickets; none of them even remotely matched those recorded in the notebook. The glaring difference was that the serial numbers on all lottery tickets started with a single letter followed by a number, whereas the notebook had two alphabets at the end of the number. This revelation brought me back to square one.

CRACKING THE CODE

My doubts were fortified by the thought that these numbers might be codes for some group members or gang that Farooq might be connected to. Without giving up, I conceived a plan to decipher the code to establish the identity of at least a few of the seven individuals; this would be sufficient to solve the mystery. The notebook was the only feeble clue pushing the investigation forward and offering a hope of some possible future breakthrough. I checked the already compiled list of Farooq's relatives, friends, acquaintances, schoolmates and batchmates to find if any name in the list matched anyone in the diary but was disappointed to find none except Mohammad Yusuf Mir. I revised and reframed the list of his relatives and friends by mixing the seven mysterious names with different serial numbers. While questioning Farooq's elder brother, I placed the list of names before him and asked him to mark the persons known to him. This was my last gamble, and my heart was pounding. After going through all the names, he picked out only Abdul Gaffar Bhat. 'Sir, he is our cousin. After giving up his studies, he established a pharmacy in his village, Hajin Sonawari,' he said casually. I did not show any excitement at his disclosure. No other name among the seven could be identified by him or any other person questioned by us. I was happy because this fresh input provided us with at least a clue to work with. Without losing any time, a special team was deputed to secure Gaffar's location.

SHOCKING REVELATIONS

After a few hours, Gaffar stood before me in my office. Even without speaking to him, I guessed he was in his late twenties and of limited intellect—a simpleton. While observing him, I could see a lot of fear in his eyes. I asked him to take a seat. With reluctance and fear, he sat on the edge of the chair, avoiding looking me in the eye. All this added to my suspicions about him. After making him comfortable, I started asking routine questions about his family, relatives, friends, education, profession, etc. to relax him and relieve his fear. I did not mention Farooq's name or the entry in the notebook, as I wanted to keep him guessing about our objective. Because I questioned him politely and gently, he seemed to shed his fear. Without waiting for further questions, he voluntarily spoke out of turn. 'Sir, I will speak the truth and the whole truth as per my knowledge. However, I fear that after I conclude, you will not believe that I have fully disclosed whatever I know. You will suspect me of withholding facts and will pressurize me to divulge more, but I will not be able to say anything more, as I do not know anything beyond what I am going to tell you.' We were startled. He seemed to be genuinely opening up. After I reassured him, he started talking with ease. What he disclosed was not only shocking to me and my team but will also surprise my readers. His statement shifted the entire narrative of the bank robbery to what I call an ideological crime, drastically altering the course of our investigation. None of us in our wildest dreams could have imagined what he disclosed. Suddenly, we realized that the bank robbery was not committed by ordinary criminals for personal gain but by a group of highly dedicated, educated, trained and ideologically motivated youth with the aim and objective of launching organized guerrilla warfare against the Indian state as per a well-drafted and exhaustive written action plan.

UNBELIEVABLE BUT TRUE

According to Gaffar, when he was a student at the Government Degree College in Sopore in north Kashmir a few years ago, Farooq would often visit him on the weekends for a night's stay at the house of Haji Mohammad Shaban Dar, a prominent businessman of Sopore, where Gaffar was staying to pursue his studies. In fact, Haji Shaban Dar was related to Farooq and Gaffar as Farooq's phuphi (father's sister) was married to Haji. According to Gaffar, Farooq would usually talk about himself, his friends, relatives, studies, hostel life, etc. during his weekend visits. However, during one of his visits, when they had gone for a long walk, Farooq asked him, 'Gaffar, hum ghulam hain ya azaad?' (Are we free people or subjugated?) 'We are subjugated by India,' Gaffar replied. 'Then why don't we do something to get freedom from India?' Farooq asked him. 'What can we do?' Gaffar asked. Farooq told him that he would find out about the plan at the appropriate time and abruptly ended the conversation; Gaffar also did not take it very seriously. He almost forgot all about what Farooq had told him until a few months later when one of his batchmates at the Government Degree College, Sopore, Ghulam Nabi Mir who hailed from Dardapora, Kupwara, asked him more or less the same questions. Mir further informed him that there was already an organization that was ready to fight for freedom. At Mir's insistence, Gaffar enlisted himself as a member of the unknown organization after signing an Oath Form with his blood, as instructed.

Gaffar further said that after some time, he received a message from Farooq to come to Srinagar to meet him at the medical college gate at a specified time. As soon as Gaffar reached there, Farooq came out to meet him. Without uttering a word, Farooq slapped him hard across the face and asked him why he had signed the Oath Form at the insistence of his classmate when Farooq had already discussed the subject with him. 'That man could be an intelligence agency's contact and the existence of the whole organization could be jeopardized because of your foolishness,' Farooq had thundered. After Farooq had unleashed his anger, Gaffar apologized and promised to be cautious in the future. At the same time, Gaffar was amazed as he realized that Farooq was a top leader of an underground organization. How else could he have come to know about his enrolment as a member of the secret organization? After Farooq calmed down, he invited Gaffar to the medical college hostel at Bamina to stay the night.

THE MYSTERIOUS GUEST

Before going to bed, Farooq informed Gaffar that he had to leave very early in the morning. 'After I leave, a guest will come to meet you. Do not question him or make any inquiries. Just listen to him carefully,' Farooq instructed. The next morning, Gaffar was still asleep when Farooq left. When he woke up, he saw a person already sitting in the room. Embarrassed, he hurriedly got out of the bed and joined him as he thought he must be the guest Farooq had told him about. The guest introduced himself as Rahman (not his real name) and seemed to be a non-Kashmiri from across the border. Rahman explained to Gaffar the objectives of the secret organization he had joined. He briefly acquainted him with the plan and educated him about the various stages, the first being recruitment; the ultimate aim was to launch a full-fledged guerrilla war against India. Their plan also envisaged kidnapping and assassinating VIPs. Rahman was consulting written notes while he explained the deadly plan to Gaffar, who was shaken to his core by the very thought of kidnapping and assassinating VIPs, waging guerrilla warfare and other frightening stuff.

As soon as Rahman left, Gaffar hurriedly walked out of the room and returned to his village without meeting Farooq. According to him, a strange fear had gripped him. He was shocked because he was not mentally prepared to take part in this dangerous game. He was so fearful and overwhelmed by what Rahman had told him that he gave up the idea of being part of this organization. He got busy with his newly established pharmacy and never looked back. Gaffar concluded his startling disclosures by stating that he had no further knowledge about the organization. He knew nothing about Rahman's antecedents or Farooq's whereabouts. When my staff tried to pressurize him for more details, he reminded them that he had told us at the outset about his inability to state more than what he knew. I was satisfied with the full disclosure of facts within his knowledge. He had no reason to conceal anything after disclosing so much dangerous information. Thereafter, he was not pressed for more information. With Gaffar's confession, we had pushed past the dead end. Now we had enough material to work out bigger issues, including the bank robbery. Gaffer's disclosure changed the discourse about the nature of the case, as it was now established to be the work of a guerrilla organization with a bigger goal. Despite the important disclosures made by Gaffar, we could not get any information from him regarding the whereabouts of Farooq and his accomplices. Gaffar was also unable to shed light on Rahman's real identity, the critical character introduced by him. We faced a vital question: where do we go from here?

THE LAST CARD

The last card that I had kept close to my chest was my guest, the paanwalla's son, Mohammad Yusuf Mir, who had 'volunteered' to help me but had not disclosed anything worthwhile. Now armed with Gaffer's vital disclosures, it was the right time to tackle him. By this time, it was midnight on the sixteenth day of our investigation. As Yusuf was available in the JIC, I called him to my room and started talking to him one-on-one, reminding him of my friendly relations with his father. I questioned him methodically, in a sustained manner. Yusuf was my last bet now. His silence would be catastrophic and would lead to my utter failure as an investigator. His questioning lasted almost the entire night of 16 January 1971. I took care not to confront him about Gaffar or the contents of his statement, as that could alert him regarding the extent of his disclosures. I wanted more than what Gaffar had disclosed. Had I even only hinted about Gaffar, I could not have extracted any useful information from Yusuf. Confronting a suspect with his co-accused or a witness is always fraught with negative consequences. Both can converse with each other even through an exchange of glances. In such a case, the whole truth would be out of reach.

When cornered by my questions, he unwittingly blurted out some useful clues about the bank robbery, though he did not admit to having participated in the actual operation. I was overjoyed when he disclosed the names of all those involved in the bank robbery, which I started noting down. Suddenly, he dropped a bomb, 'Why are you writing the names? These are only code names,' he said. My head swirled. 'What are their real names? Come on, tell me quickly. I don't have much time now,' I thundered in desperation. 'Sir, I don't know their real names,' he replied coolly, adding to my frustration. I got up to control my anger and despair. I paced up and down the room in a bid to calm my nerves. Then I sat down again facing him and told him, 'Look, whatever you have disclosed is sufficient to conclude that you are a senior member of the organization, and as such, you know the whole story. Now tell me where Farooq is at this point of time.' I tried a different move to finally floor him. No code name needed to be decoded, and no time was to be wasted, I decided. 'In the safe house,' he dropped another bomb very calmly. The use of the term 'safe house' by a boy in his teens startled me. However, with this word, a bell rang in my head, and I discovered this unassuming character's strategic knowledge about guerrilla warfare. 'What safe house? Where?' I asked hurriedly. 'At Barsoo,' he said. 'Whose house?' I asked impatiently as I did not believe my ears about what he was saying. 'Our house. We built it with the money looted by our organization from the District Education Office, Pulwama, in April 1970.' With each word uttered by him, I was getting more excited and impatient. 'Come on. Show me the place. You will accompany me to the safe house,' I said to him to test the truthfulness of his claim. He agreed reluctantly. I was happy at the probability that we might also be able to crack the Pulwama Dacoity case.

THE SAFE HOUSE

At this stage, I rang up my boss, the DIG of police, Kashmir Range, and told him there had been a real breakthrough, requesting him to come urgently. He arrived in no time, and after discussing and analysing all the information gathered from Gaffar and Yusuf, we planned an operation to raid the mysterious safe house. Guided by Yusuf and with a platoon of armed police, we reached Barsoo, a village about 20 km from Pulwama on the Srinagar–Jammu National Highway. He pointed to the safe house that was facing the highway and had its backyard towards the slope of the right bank of the river Jhelum. The house was situated about 100 yards away from the village in an almost isolated spot with no structures in its immediate proximity. We laid a cordon around the boundary wall of the house and carefully approached it from the rear without arousing the suspicion of the occupants. Not a soul was visible anywhere outside or inside the house. As soon as we approached the rear wall, the occupants, who may have noticed us from inside, opened fire; we cautiously retaliated using the boundary wall as our shield. Our plan was to get them alive.

During the exchange of fire, I shouted at them to come out and surrender. 'You have been surrounded from all sides. You have no chance of escape. No harm will come to you. Your safety is guaranteed. Come out.' I kept shouting at them in the midst of firing, which attracted some villagers, including the numberdar and chowkidar. After a while, there was a pause in the firing from the house. The rear door of the house opened slowly and two individuals came out with their hands up, without any weapons. We rushed into the compound, swiftly apprehended them and secured their custody. One of them was Farooq, whom we recognized from his photograph on the college admission form. The other person, who was in his thirties, introduced himself as Nazir Ahmed Wani, an agriculture assistant in the state's agriculture department. Part of the cash, amounting to ₹8,600 that was looted from J&K Bank, was recovered from the ground floor room. Some important documents, including microfilms and highly classified Indian army manuals with printed warnings on the cover, 'THIS DOCUMENT MUST NOT FALL INTO ENEMY HANDS', were recovered from the same room. Equipment capable of being used for espionage was also recovered.

CODE NAMES

Neither of them addressed each other by their real names. Nazir Ahmed Wani, who had assumed the code name of Assad, was known to the locals as the domestic servant of the 'contractors' living in the house, performing all their household errands. Farooq was called Suhail. Yusuf Mir, known as Tariq, remained in our well-guarded vehicle throughout the operation. Farooq and Nazir were whisked away from the spot along with the seized money and other items.

THE TRAP

The safe house was put under close but unobtrusive surveillance, and a trap was laid inside with a couple of our officers disguised as villagers. At about midday, a young man entered the house. Once apprehended, he disclosed his name to be Fazal Haq Qureshi; Abdullah was his code name. He was one of the important leaders and a founding member of the organization. He was also hurriedly taken into custody. Another person who walked into the trap after a while was Abdul Hai, code-named Aslam, a young man from Doda. He was carrying a small container of pure ghee as a gift for his senior associates. The recurring success we encountered made our day. Questioning the arrested individuals at the JIC led us to another safe house rented by the organization in Shaheed Gunj in southern Srinagar, near the Old Secretariat. None other than Ghulam Rasool Zahgir, known by his code name Rahman, one of the founding leaders and the kingpin of the organization, was reportedly holed up here.

ZAHGIR, THE SUPREMO

As we have seen in an earlier story (Red Kashmir), Zahgir was allegedly involved in the killing of Constable Charan Dass, a BSF sentry guarding Nawa Kadal Bridge, in the city's interiors on 3 February 1967. This was the first act of insurgency in the state. It was Zahgir who had briefed Gaffar in Farooq's medical college hostel room under his code name Rahman.

The Shaheed Gunj safe house was raided the same night by a police party headed by me and assisted by another colleague, Abdul Majid Lone. A strategy evolved on the spot with a view to not attract the attention of the occupants of the three-storey building or neighbours in the locality; we silently scaled up the high boundary wall and climbed through a window to reach the first floor of the safe house. Though we knew that Zahgir was armed and may open fire at any time, we had no option but to take the risk. He was believed to be in a room on the third floor. We broke open the door with a collective push. As the door collapsed, we barged into the room and crouched into a lying down position to protect ourselves against any firing by him. I quickly moved towards his bed where he was calmly sitting, leaning against the backrest under a quilt with the lights on. Suspecting him to be armed, I quickly grabbed both his hands. 'I don't have a weapon with me,' he said pointing to his loaded revolver in his jacket hanging from a peg on the wall above his head.

Numerous vital documents, including the final list of the members of the organization and ₹12,000 in cash, were recovered. Surprisingly, Zahgir did not resist arrest and accompanied us with a smile. I was seeing him for the first time because till then, his subversive activities had been investigated either by the local police or CI. We escorted him down the stairs and out of the safe house. There was complete silence around as none of the neighbours had woken up and the roads were deserted. I took the wheel of the jeep while Zahgir sat in the middle, between me and another officer. While sitting next to me absolutely relaxed, I asked him why he did not resist or fire at us despite being armed with a loaded revolver. 'While sitting on the bed, I heard some feeble sounds and guessed that it was a police raid. I instantly concluded that all the important members of the group except me had been arrested. I was the last one, as my present location was known to none other than Abdullah (Fazal Haq),' he replied. Talking in a relaxed manner in the moving vehicle, he asked for my opinion, 'Which of the two operations was better planned—Pulwama or Hazratbal?' 'Obviously, Pulwama,' I said. 'It was a very well-planned operation that left behind no trace or even a slight clue,' I replied. 'Pulwama was planned by me and Hazratbal by Nazir Ahmed Wani,' he said. Nazir was a rash person. The investigation that followed revealed that the J&K Bank Hazratbal robbery had indeed been executed by Nazir Ahmed Wani dressed as a deputy SP, Farooq Ahmed Bhat as an inspector and Nissar Hussain Mir of Anantnag and Abdul Hai of Doda as constables.

MY CUNNING GUEST

I spoke to Farooq at the JIC regarding the stolen cash. Notwithstanding the fact that all the important members of the organization had been arrested, a major portion of the stolen amount had not been recovered. By that time, we had only recovered a small amount of stolen money from the Barsoo safe house and from Zahgir's possession. When asked about it, Farooq broke down and cried bitterly; he was unable to utter a word. I hugged him and tried to console him. 'Sir, my father wanted me to be a doctor, but look what I have made of myself: a criminal, a robber. Now I shall never become a doctor,' he lamented while sobbing uncontrollably. Consoling him, I reassured him, 'Don't worry. I am sure that someday you will become a doctor.' After he relaxed, I asked him, 'Where is the stolen money?' 'Didn't Tariq tell you? The cash is with him,' he replied. I was shocked. After his sixteen days' stay with me, his offer to help me and his thorough questioning the previous night, Tariq had not even hinted that the stolen money was in his possession. 'What a cunning hard nut! He really is a dedicated guy,' I thought. When I asked Yusuf about why he had not informed me that the money was with him, he said, 'Jenab, yeh ghar ki baat hai. Main kabhi bhi aap ko cash dey sakta tha.' (Sir, this is a family matter. I could have given you the cash anytime.) What an excuse! Without any hesitation, he disclosed that the rest of the cash was concealed in the attic of his father's house in Gogji Bagh, Srinagar. A police party personally headed by the DIG Kashmir recovered ₹70,000 concealed in the ceiling of the attic of his father's house. Thus, of the total stolen amount of ₹97,175.75, we recovered ₹91,321. The rest of the money had been used to purchase equipment and gadgets for the collection, and for preservation and dissemination of vital intelligence to Pakistan's army authorities.

A HUMANITARIAN APPROACH

During the investigation, Peer Mohammad Hussain, one of the members of Al Fatah from Kadapora, Anantnag, was apprehended in Srinagar. As he was brought to the JIC, he seemed tense and extremely fearful. He told me about his infant daughter's serious illness and how he had purchased some life-saving drugs for her. In utter desperation and out of fear of losing his daughter, he requested me to allow him to deliver the medicines to his home. 'I will come back soon,' he said. I allowed him to go but decided to send an officer with him in a government vehicle, to ensure the safe delivery of the medicines and Hussain's return to the JIC. It is believed that the baby has now grown into adulthood, possibly even becoming a mother-in-law. Hussain, who was already in government service, pursued his career and retired as a mid-level bureaucrat. He was so close to Mufti Mohammad Sayeed—the supremo of the People's Democratic Party (PDP)—that he got inducted in his ministry. However, after Mufti's demise, Hussain joined the NC.

AL FATAH WIPED OUT

Starting in the early hours of 16 January 1971, the whole organizational set-up of Al Fatah was dismantled through police operations within 24 hours. The case was resolved in only 16 days. The arrest of Zahgir and the other leaders led to the arrest of about 200 enlisted members across the Valley and in Doda and Kishtwar in Jammu. Luckily, Zahgir had maintained a complete list of the members of Al Fatah. The name was given to the organization after Zahgir and Fazal returned from Pakistan in January 1969 where they had received training and the blueprint for building a formidable guerrilla outfit in the state. However, they had not disclosed it to their cadres to prevent any leaks.

SAFE HOUSE OWNERSHIP

It may be recalled that during the course of the investigation we came to know about the existence of a safe house in Barsoo on the Srinagar–Jammu National Highway for the first time from Yusuf Mir. During the investigation, it was disclosed that the house had been built by Zahgir and his associates using the booty of the Pulwama dacoity, which was for exclusive use by their organization. The money from the dacoity was used to purchase a piece of land as well as to construct a modest house on the national highway. The sale deed of the land was executed and registered in the name of one Mohammad Shafi Peerzada from Bandipora, a relative of Fazal Haq. A small amount had been given to Abdul Hai of Doda to set up a tea shop in his town to serve as a cover and also as a rendezvous point for the members of the organization without arousing any suspicion. A poultry farm was also set up in Bijbehara to create more resources for the organization. Besides the Barsoo house, Al Fatah had hired rented private houses in Anantnag, Shaheed Gunj, Buchwara and Khona Khan Dalgate in Srinagar to be used as safe houses. The accused assembled at, held consultations and went to commit the Hazratbal bank robbery from the Khona Khan safe house.

HUNT FOR ARMS

Having traced such a lethal organization, we were intrigued by the absence of arms and ammunition except for a few pistols and some grenades, which were buried in the courtyard of the Barsoo safe house and seized after the raid on Zahgir's insistence. It was beyond comprehension how they could plan an armed struggle without a substantial quantity of arms and ammunition. We suspected that Zahgir, Fazal Haq and Nazir Wani, the founding leaders of Al Fatah, had not fully disclosed the truth to us or that they might have been in the process of acquiring arms from Pakistan or some other source. According to them, Pakistani authorities had promised to provide arms at the appropriate time but to our knowledge, no arms had been supplied in bulk yet. The Pakistani army and intelligence officers had instructed the organization leadership to grow as an indigenous outfit by creating their own resources. In pursuit of this objective, the organization had resorted to committing criminal acts to generate financial resources. It may be recalled that one of their sister organizations had attempted to rob the Islamia College, Srinagar, armoury that had dummy guns for the training of NCC cadets, but failed.

LOCAL TRAINING CENTRE

Further investigations revealed that Zahgir and Fazal Haq Qureshi had come in contact with the veteran spy and courier, Jahangir Khan, as a jail mate after his arrest in 1961 and had discussed their plans with him. He had generally promised to help them in whatever manner they wanted. After Jahangir Khan was acquitted in the Srinagar Bomb Case, the Al Fatah leaders organized training camps with his help for some of their recruits in the Haka Khal forests near Arizal, tehsil Beerwah. They used locally manufactured dummy weapons, and Jahangir Khan served as a trainer. He had already established a poultry farm in Haka Khal as a cover for his renewed covert activities to aid Al Fatah. Khan had assured Zahgir that sufficient weapons would be provided to Al Fatah at the proper time.

PAKISTANI SPY

To clarify this important aspect and unearth more clues about the supply or existence of arms, Zahgir was questioned again. He disclosed that after the Pulwama Education Office Dacoity, Mufti Zia-u-Din, originally a resident of Kreeri in Baramulla district, had come from Pakistan. A well-known figure of his times, Mufti had migrated to Pakistan immediately after Partition. He was visiting Kashmir for the first time on a proper visa and had been instructed by Pakistani Army authorities to contact Zahgir to find out how much progress Al Fatah had made. Zahgir and Fazal Haq met with him in Kreeri and briefed him about the organization's progress. They informed him that the organization was ready for guerrilla attacks but lacked arms and ammunition. Mufti reportedly told them that the weapons would be made available to them at the appropriate time. He told them to wait for further instructions.

ARMS CACHE

Meanwhile, with a growing desire to acquire arms, Zahgir again turned to Jahangir Khan and pressed him to arrange arms as promised. Jahangir Khan disclosed to him that arms were cached with Haji Jalal-ud-Din, an aged and respected person from Charar-e-Sharief in central Kashmir. However, he warned Zahgir not to approach Haji without authorization from Pakistani authorities. That is why Zahgir never contacted Haji.

In the section on the Srinagar Bomb Case, it was disclosed that around 1948, loads of arms and ammunition were brought into the Valley by some accused persons, especially Jahangir Khan. Jalal-ud-Din had been an active member of a subversive organization that had its headquarters in Poonch. Despite being arrested, none of the members of the organization had ever disclosed the actual location of the arms cache.

With this background, Haji Jalal-ud-Din posed a fresh challenge to us. Once Haji's name was disclosed by Zahgir, we innocuously secured his presence at the JIC after taking his son, a serving police officer, into confidence. He too was unaware of Haji's past. Haji was a frail old ailing man of over 80 years. It was very difficult to talk to him, let alone interrogate him in custody. However, we had no alternative but to lay our hands on the lethal stuff allegedly in his possession. He was made comfortable with all the facilities required by a man of his age, including medical aid, comfortable bedding, food of his choice and a separate room at the JIC. He was made to feel at home and quizzed very tactfully and professionally while maintaining a friendly atmosphere.

Each question was properly articulated to avoid causing him any discomfort. One of our Sikh officers even voluntarily performed the custom of washing his feet every evening with hot water, as is common among the elderly in the Valley, particularly in the winter. Our personalized and polite handling of the old man paid dividends. He disclosed that the pony-loads of arms smuggled into the Valley from Pakistan in 1948 had been entrusted to him for safekeeping until further instructions from some reliable Pakistani agency. He said that he had been repeatedly interrogated on this account. He had been also arrested in the early 1950s and interrogated at the Red Fort interrogation centre in Delhi, but he never disclosed the secret to anyone. Haji was highly dedicated and committed to the Pakistani ideology.

That is why he had been able to keep this secret for over two decades without even hinting at it to his own family.

Though Haji offered to personally accompany us and hand over the arms, I refused his offer for fear of a possible hostile public reaction. I suggested he help us make a site plan of the exact spot where the arms were cached. Haji provided the details, revealing that the weapons were cached in his own house, with some hand grenades buried in the adjacent kitchen garden. Haji disclosed that the weapons were hidden in the top end of the wall in the attic of his four-storey palatial house, covered with mud plaster just under the sloping roof. We were very cautious as we could not afford to have our operations prematurely leaked; it would jeopardize our chances of getting to the hidden treasure of weapons smuggled from Pakistan into the Valley more than two decades ago. However, with Haji's cooperation, we prepared a rough building plan of his house and he pinpointed the exact spot where the arms and ammunition were cached.

As we discreetly reached the town in the early hours of the morning, we contacted Haji's police officer. He accompanied us to the attic of the house as instructed. Just below the sloping corrugated tin sheet roof, we removed the mud plaster covering the deep cavity of the wall at the spot accurately marked in our rough plan. Everyone present, including Haji's family members, was stunned to see the huge stockpile of arms in front of them. We recovered 12 carbine sten guns, .38 revolvers, 24 magazines and 390 rounds of ammunition. Haji's family members were shocked as they had no knowledge of such a huge consignment of arms cached in their house. His police officer son told us that his father used to discourage family members, including children, from going up to the attic, warning them that the place was haunted and inhabited by a jinn (tasrufdar in Kashmiri) who may harm them. After taking possession of the arms, we decided to abandon the digging of the kitchen garden for the recovery of hand grenades. We feared that if the rusted hand grenades were struck by our digging tools, they might explode and result in the death or injury of those present. Additionally, digging in broad daylight would have also attracted the attention of the neighbours in the densely populated locality who could have attacked us to protect the cached hand grenades. Upon returning to Srinagar, the arms were cleaned and polished by professional armourers and found fit for use. This was the first, and perhaps the last, single largest recovery of arms from an underground organization in the state. Subsequently, one .303 gun was also recovered from Farooq.

SURVEY BEFORE THE BANK ROBBERY

Before deciding to rob the J&K Bank at Hazratbal, Al Fatah operatives had surveyed many banks and very closely studied the managers' character, personality and behaviour. The manager of Hazratbal Bank was zeroed in on because of his apparent simplicity and gullibility. The Al Fatah operatives had also collected information in advance about the amount of cash that would be drawn by the manager from the State Bank of India, Residency Road, Srinagar, on the morning of the robbery. Similarly, before committing the Pulwama dacoity, they had done a lot of homework to ensure that their plans could be carried out smoothly.

HIGH-PROFILE RECRUITMENT

Recruitment into the organization was so meticulous that no one could be recruited randomly, as is common in other political or even underground organizations. Anybody interested in joining Al Fatah had to be introduced by a senior member of the organization. Nazir Ahmed Wani was supposed to verify the character and antecedents of all such aspirants. The antecedents checked included the aspirant's family background, including if any family member was in government service, particularly in the police, CID or any other intelligence organization. Family members' political affiliations would also be ascertained and recorded. An aspirant who had any relatives in the police or CID or was affiliated to a pro-India political party would not be admitted to the organization. Only those who were cleared by Nazir after thorough verification were admitted, subject to their agreement to sign an oath in blood.

Though around 200 members had been recruited to Al Fatah by January 1970, only about 40 had been indoctrinated. They were trained and ready to take up guerrilla operations. Some of them were also trained in various other aspects, such as espionage, coding and deciphering radio messages. They were well-versed in espionage principles, such as shunning surveillance and the policy of 'need to know', commonly used by spies, undercover agents and members of secret resistance outfits worldwide. They were also familiar with the ideologies of Cuban revolutionary leaders, namely, Che Guevara, whose book *Guerrilla Warfare* they had read, and Fidel Castro.

PAKISTANI DIPLOMAT

Zafar Iqbal Rathore, the Pakistan Intelligence Bureau officer, to whom Zahgir, Nazir and Fazal Haq had been introduced in Pakistan, had been posted as first secretary at the PHC in New Delhi as part of the plan to handle Al Fatah. Their handlers in Pakistan had informed Al Fatah about Rathore's upcoming posting in Delhi. After exposing Rathore as the handler of Al Fatah, a comprehensive report was directly sent by IGP Surendra Nath to Prime Minister Indira Gandhi. Rathore was declared 'persona non grata' by the GoI and directed to leave the country immediately.

PULWAMA DACOITY

According to the blueprint provided by Pakistani intelligence and army authorities to Zahgir and the other leaders, Al Fatah had to create its own financial resources. Therefore, they initially decided to rob the government treasury in Anantnag but later abandoned the project due to the presence of armed guards. In the absence of proper arms, they were not in a position to face and fight the well-trained guards even though the guards were only armed with obsolete .303 rifles. Ultimately, the Al Fatah members zeroed in on the education department office in Pulwama and decided to commit the robbery on the night after pay day. From a team of 15 members, only 10 were selected for the actual operation. The rest were detailed to keep watch around the target office. Besides Zahgir and Farooq Ahmed Bhat, the team of 10 comprised Nissar Husain, Bashir Ahmed, Ghulam Hassan Shakhsaz, Hamidullah, and Mohammad Sayed Khan, from Anantnag, as well as Iqbal Beg, a law student from Doda studying in Jammu, and Iqbal Hashia and Mohammad Iqbal Sheikh from Kishtwar.

On 1 April 1970, the cashier of the target office drew the salary of the employees from the Pulwama treasury. One Al Fatah member, Saleem Gilkar of Anantnag, was deputed to keep an eye on the cashier while the pay was being dispersed to keep track of the disbursements made during the day, ensuring that sufficient cash was available even after such disbursement. Satisfied that a substantial amount of cash remained, the group decided to strike on the night of 2 April 1970. Farooq was deputed to steal a vehicle (an uncommon crime in those days in Kashmir) to facilitate their escape after the operation. Accordingly, Farooq stole a jeep parked at Lal Chowk, Srinagar, belonging to one Abdul Aziz Haroon, a resident of the Barbar Shah locality of Srinagar. Farooq drove the stolen jeep to Anantnag the same night as commanded by Zahgir. The members of the organization selected for the operation by Zahgir, who had assembled at a safe house (a rented building in Anantnag), were picked up and taken to Pulwama in the stolen jeep. Zahgir and Farooq were armed with revolvers, whereas the others had daggers and other weapons. The education office was guarded by three unarmed chowkidars who were silenced and threatened with a show of arms. One of them, who seemed somewhat defiant, was silenced by placing a chloroform-soaked handkerchief on his mouth and nostrils. The chemical had been procured by Mohammad Sayed Khan.

The Al Fatah guerrillas brought down the huge locked iron chest and loaded it into the stolen jeep. They hurriedly drove down the Pulwama–Koil–Awantipora road and took the Srinagar–Jammu National Highway to reach Bijbehara, where they turned left towards the Bijbehara–Langanbal–Pahalgam road and dumped the safe under a culvert near Srigufwara village. The jeep was later abandoned at Dantar, a village near Anantnag. The next morning, they hired the services of a mechanic from Anantnag named Gul Mohammad, who later assumed the name Gul Rafeeqi as a mainstream politician. He was elected on an NC ticket in 1996. Gul skilfully broke open the safe from which ₹71,847.60—quite a handsome amount in those days—was recovered and taken. The perpetrators of the crime vanished without leaving behind any trace.

CASE CLOSED AS UNTRACED

The case was taken up by the district police of Anantnag for investigation. It was the first armed dacoity of its type in the Valley and an unprecedented sensational crime by all standards. Besides being treated as a pure crime by the district police, CI sleuths probed its possible political dimensions as well. The Naxalbari uprising of 1967, subsequently taken over by the Communist Party of India (Marxist–Leninist) in 1969, was at its peak in West Bengal. Naxalite cadres were ideologically committed to their leaders Charu Majumdar, Kanu Sanyal and Jangal Santhal, and allegedly looted government offices, treasuries, banks, etc. in various parts of the country, especially West Bengal. Led by Ram Piara Saraf, a freedom fighter and Jammu-based leftist leader, there was a small group of this organization in Jammu & Kashmir also.[9] Previously, Saraf had been jailed in 1945 along with his colleague Krishan Dev Sethi for actively participating in the Quit Kashmir agitation launched by Sheikh Abdullah against Maharaja Hari Singh. They were part of the NC's communist wing. However, the communists also backstabbed Sheikh in August 1953.

The police team was headed by Badri Nath Kotru, the district SP of Anantnag, who probed all possible lines of investigation but were unsuccessful in unravelling the mystery. CM Ghulam Mohammed Sadiq was so concerned about this unprecedented crime that he would inquire about its progress whenever the IGP and DIG met him, much to their embarrassment. Driven up the

---

[9]Express News Service, 'Last Surviving Member of J&K Constituent Assembly Dies in Jammu, *The Indian Express*, 28 January 2021, https://indianexpress.com/article/cities/jammu/last-surviving-member-of-jk-constituent-assembly-dies-in-jammu-7165130/. Accessed on 9 February 2024.

wall, Kotru reportedly proposed a solution to the IGP. He told him that all the burglars, criminals and known bad characters of the district were fed up with repeated calls, questioning and harassment by the police for almost a year. As a compromise, they had offered to collectively contribute the stolen amount to be shown as recovered from a few of them. They had also assured him that they would confess their 'crime' before the court and accept the sentence. IGP Surendra Nath, who was an upright, shrewd and professional police officer, instantly rejected Kotru's unprofessional proposal. The IGP had reportedly told him that his suggestion would amount to self-deception as those actually responsible for this sensational crime would laugh at the police and be encouraged to commit many more such crimes in the future. The IGP asked him to leave the case as it was and close it as untraced.

During one of his visits to the JIC to assess the progress of the investigation before the final breakthrough, I had assured Surendra Nath, 'Sir, God willing, I will produce three aces.' By solving the Pulwama Dacoity, Hazratbal Bank Robbery and Lal Chowk Jeep Theft, my team and I produced the real 'Three Aces'.

UNAWARE SISTER AGENCIES

All the arrests of the Al Fatah members and the recoveries made were well-guarded secrets, even though arrests were made not only in the Valley but also in Jammu, Doda and Kishtwar over two weeks. It was such a well-planned and professional job carried out by a dedicated team of officers that neither the media nor our sister intelligence agencies found out about these operations. The intelligence agencies of the GoI based in the Valley were unaware of our operations, so much so that Mathur, the then resident Deputy Director of IB at Srinagar and Surendra Nath's batchmate, complained to him for not taking him into confidence before sending a report to the Prime Minister. Later, the IB deputed a special team of interrogators from New Delhi to verify our findings. The team also included some veteran Red Fort interrogators. After getting clearance from our chief, they met with me. I allowed them free access to all the arrested members of Al Fatah who fully cooperated with them. After they were done interrogating them, they called on me again and started picking holes, particularly regarding the infiltration route along the Ramgarh border of Jammu, which, according to them, was impregnable. They tried to negate facts and were hell-bent on creating doubts about Al Fatah operatives crossing and recrossing the international border at will. I could easily understand the game they were trying to play. I advised them to recommend a probe by a Supreme Court judge so that the concerned army commanders were taken to task for their lapses and negligence. I am recording this only to show how sister agencies at the centre, only to satisfy their ego or to cover up their shortcomings, tried to play games and question the veracity of our investigation, which had implications for the security of the state.

ARMY ADVICE OVERRULED

Once the investigation was concluded, some senior army officers suggested that the ringleaders of Al Fatah and those who had participated in criminal acts should be deported to PoK through the CFL under the provisions of the Egress and Internal Movement Control Ordinance (E&IMCO). As an alternative, they suggested that the accused persons be branded and condemned as simple criminals. However, the J&K Police dismissed these suggestions and told them that the full and true story would be disclosed in the chargesheet to be filed against them in a court of law. We argued that concealing the real objective of the organization would amount to the deliberate suppression of the truth regarding the prevailing security in the state, which would have far-reaching adverse consequences.

TORTURED BOY

Mohammad Iqbal Beg, one of the accused let off by the high court, was a law student at the Jammu Law College. He figured as one of the accused in the Pulwama Dacoity Case. Therefore, I requested Thakur Gandarab Singh (on deputation from Punjab Police) then SP, CID Special Branch, Jammu, to secure his presence and send him to JIC Srinagar. However, due to my busy schedule, I forgot about the arrangement. After a week or so, I realized that Iqbal Beg had not been sent to Srinagar. I rang up the SP CID, who told me that Iqbal had been arrested and was being interrogated. I lost my temper and told the SP, 'Who are you to question him? On what basis are you doing so when you don't know anything about his involvement? I am the investigating officer. You have no right to interfere. Send him to me today or I will inform the IGP about your unnecessary meddling and sabotaging the investigation.' My threat worked, and the same evening I was informed that Iqbal had arrived at JIC Srinagar. I told the orderly to bring him to me. A lean and thin young boy was ushered in. He was shivering, not due to the cold but out of fear. A sort of freezing fear had gripped him. Pointing to a sofa, I asked him to sit down. He hesitated and continued shivering. I again asked him to sit down. He started crying loudly; tears rolled down his cheeks. I asked him why he was crying. I wondered if any of my staff had misbehaved with him. He continued to weep inconsolably without uttering a word. I got up, held his hands and made him sit on the sofa, but he didn't stop crying. I asked my staff whether they had asked him anything or roughed him up. They all denied and said that he had just arrived when he was brought to me. Besides, nobody could question any suspect without my authorization. The use of third-degree methods was strictly prohibited in our investigation. I called for tea, but he refused to have it. On my insistence, he held the cup, but his shivering was so intense that his cup was about to slip from his hand. I got up, took the cup from his hand and asked him to relax. I sat with him and tried to console him. When he was a bit relaxed, I asked him, 'What is the matter? Why are you so scared? You have nothing to fear. You are safe here.' I assured him that nobody was going to touch him.

Relaxing a bit, he narrated a horrible and inhuman tale of torture and third-degree treatment by the SP CID and his staff at Jammu for a week after his arrest. 'Sir, after my arrest in Jammu, I was continuously tortured physically and mentally to extract a confession from me. They tortured me in every possible manner and locked me up in a stinking latrine where the foul smell almost suffocated me. Since then, I haven't got even a wink of sleep,' he said while crying and on the verge of collapsing. However, after he had had a cup of tea at my insistence, he relaxed a bit. I asked him to rest and sleep for some time. One of the orderlies was asked to provide him with bedding and a room to sleep in. Though Iqbal had offered to make a statement, I simply sent him to his room. We did not question him about his involvement for a couple of days. There was no hurry either because we already knew what he would state, including his role in the Pulwama Dacoity. After a few days, I called him. He was happy, smiling, fresh and ready to tell whatever he knew. I asked an officer to record his statement, which, by that time, was only a formality.

PAKISTAN ACTION PLAN

Pakistani authorities had provided Zahgir and his associates with a secret blueprint to raise a guerrilla organization. The plan was to launch guerrilla attacks on the Indian army and police, as well as kidnap and assassinate political leaders. This multidimensional plan also aimed at weakening the Indian state administratively, economically, politically and militarily. The plan was explained to all the members recruited by Zahgir. During this period, the organization was named Al Fatah, inspired by the popularity of Yasser Arafat for his Palestinian liberation militant operations.

POLITICAL WING

Al Fatah's blueprint also provided for a political wing, which was established in 1970 under the unsuspecting name Young Men's League and Students' Federation. It was launched by the senior members of Al Fatah—Abdul Rashid Dar of Bulbul Nowgam, Anantnag, Mohammad Saleem Baig of Khanqah-e-Moula, Srinagar and Mohammad Yusuf Mir of Verinag, with the blessings and patronage of Mirza Afzal Beg, the head of the PF. Beg was also kept in the loop about the existence and operations of Al Fatah by Zahgir. On many occasions, Beg stopped on the Srinagar–Jammu Highway outside the Barsoo safe house, where the inmates, particularly Zahgir and Rashid Dar, would come out to meet him. The Federation mostly published and circulated anti-India posters and also captured the platform of different mosques to address the Friday gatherings to pursue their political agenda. They routinely organized violent anti-India demonstrations of students and youth in Srinagar and other major towns in the Valley on one pretext or the other, no matter how trivial.

Here, I am reminded of an interesting story about Abdul Rashid Dar. He was often wanted by the police for various reasons. In a bid to use him as an asset, IB officials were very keen on arresting him. Their agents would also watch his movements closely. Once, when I was at the Kothibagh Police Station, Rashid Dar came running into the police station. He was almost breathless and collapsed on the floor. I got up and lifted him with the help of another police officer and lifted him onto a table. While he was being given some water to drink, he whispered to me, 'Sir, I have been shot in the chest by an IB officer.' His right hand was over his chest from where blood was oozing out. We removed his shirt but did not find any injury. We found a large red stain on his white undershirt, spread due to profuse sweating. Even the alleged firing at him by an IB officer was doubtful because the IB does not have any mandate to arrest anyone. They are only supposed to inform the police whenever any wanted man is located by them. A state police or CID official might have chased him to apprehend him.

STEEP RISE

The steep rise in resistance can be attributed to the fact that over the five years from 1965 to 1970, the state police had unearthed as many as 80 underground cells, espionage outfits and subversive groups. During the same period, the police had also seized arms and lethal material from the members of the quashed underground cells; this is excluding the seizures made from Al Fatah.

.303 Rifles	231
Guns	309
Sten guns	8
Light machine guns	4
Revolvers	44
Hand grenades	431
2-inch mortar shells	66
Ammunition/Rounds	91,000
Bayonets	65
Automatic rifles	5
Magazines	21
Detonators	117
Explosives	1600 lb
Bombs	30
Rocket launchers	2
Wireless sets	3

Source: Surendra Nath's (IGP, J&K) report on seizure of arms dated 4 February 1971

The extent of the recovery of arms, ammunition, explosives and other lethal material may give a fair idea of the magnitude and potential of resistance groups to pick up arms for their cause. Our efforts undoubtedly restricted the progression of an armed uprising, but ultimately, it reared its head again and spread its tentacles in the form of militancy that has been ongoing since 1988. While dealing with militants, J&K was converted into a battle arena, significantly disadvantaging the people of the state at large.

CHARGESHEET

Apart from Zahgir, Fazal Haq, Nazir Wani and the other co-accused in the robbery and dacoity cases, Rashid Dar, Saleem Beg and Mohammad Yusuf Mir were arraigned as accused in the chargesheet filed against 22 Al Fatah members on different counts before a special judge in Central Jail, Jammu, which was later transferred to Srinagar Central Jail. The accused were represented by eminent lawyers like Mirza Afzal Beg, Piyare Lal Handoo (later an NC minister) and Iqbal Kishen Kotwal (later elevated to the bench). Almost all the witnesses were examined by the trial court. I also appeared in the special court at Srinagar Central Jail as the investigator. Instead of being shown animosity, I was treated with utmost respect not only by the accused individuals but also by the defence counsels, particularly Mirza Afzal Beg, who was extra polite and friendly while conducting my cross-examination, which lasted about two and a half months.

CASE WITHDRAWN

The trial could not be brought to its logical end after the Indira–Sheikh Accord of 1975, when Sheikh Mohammad Abdullah assumed power. Some knowledgeable political circles believe that withdrawing the case was one of the unwritten conditions of the Indira–Sheikh Accord of 1975. Had the trial continued, most of the accused would have been convicted on the basis of the scientific evidence collected during the investigation. On an application filed by Mirza Afzal Beg, three of the accused, Abdul Rashid Dar, Mohammad Saleem Baig and Mohammad Iqbal Beg of Doda, had already been let off by the High Court of J&K with the exercise of their inherent powers under section 561A of the CrPC. After his release, Dar studied law at Jammu University. Barring myself and Mirza Afzal Beg, no one was aware of his location. That is how

Rashid Dar was rehabilitated. After completing his law studies, he joined the Bar in Anantnag and started his legal practice. I was also posted there in those days. After the Indira–Sheikh Accord of 1975, he held some organizational positions in the NC and was later elected as an MLA for some terms. Subsequently, he held the position of chairman of the Legislative Council for more than one term. Owing to his constitutional position, he had the opportunity to visit many foreign countries. As chairman, he allegedly allowed the dilution of the state subject law in favour of Kashmiri women marrying non-state subjects. Abdul Rashid Dar died in March 2020. I was informed about his death in Jammu, where I was working on this book.

Saleem Beg, upon completing his studies, was hired by Revenue Minister Beg as part of his personal staff. He also quit politics, concentrated on his career as a civil servant and retired as director general of the tourism department. Presently, he is a prominent activist associated with the Indian National Trust for Art and Cultural Heritage. However, Mohammad Yusuf Mir of Verinag, another co-founder of Al Fatah's political wing, could not get any substantial benefit and continued to struggle for a livelihood. Iqbal Beg reportedly joined the revenue department as naib tehsildar and retired as a senior revenue officer. He has also reportedly passed away.

AL FATAH SPLIT

Over time, while the members were still in jail, Al Fatah developed cracks and split. Zahgir headed Inqilabi Mahaz, which supported the Indira–Sheikh Accord, whereas the other group, headed by Nazir Ahmad Wani and Fazal Haq Qureshi, rejected the Accord and decided to continue the resistance. However, members of both groups were released after the withdrawal of the case.

CAUSE OF FAILURE

Al Fatah failed because its Pakistani bosses advised the group to fend for themselves and generate their own resources. The arms and ammunition cached with Haji Jalal-ud-Din could not be accessed by them. Though a dedicated cadre of guerrillas, Al Fatah and all its covert activities could have gone undetected had it not committed crimes like auto theft, dacoity and robbery to create financial resources for their organization. Neither Al Fatah nor any of its members received any financial assistance from Pakistan or any other country or individual. It was purely an indigenous underground guerrilla outfit; it only received encouragement and strategic assistance from Pakistani army authorities. Moreover, the group's dedication was utilized by the Pakistani Army for espionage. The strategic material collected and transferred onto microfilm was handed over to Zaffar Iqbal Rathore at the PHC in New Delhi. These subsidiary activities diluted the very objective of the guerrilla organization.

DEDICATION

It will be unjust if I don't put on record that neither Zahgir nor any other member of Al Fatah misused or spent a single penny that they looted from the Pulwama Education Office or J&K Bank, Hazratbal, for their personal use. In his secret report dated 4 February 1971, IGP Surendra Nath observed the following:

> It is highly significant that the large amount that had been procured in this dacoity was utilized entirely for the purposes of the underground organization and was not distributed among the members of the gang as personal booty. This reveals a sense of dedication on the part of the members of the organization to their cause. It also provides

a reason why it was not possible to get any clue regarding this crime. Normally, criminals fall out on the distribution of the loot or due to other jealousies or rivalries. In the present case, Zahgir had kept fairly strict control and the members were satisfied in having taken part in an operation that furthered the cause of their organization.

BUSINESS VENTURE

Immediately after the withdrawal of the case, Zahgir and Yusuf Mir entered into a business partnership and were granted a forest lease for an area in Kapran, Verinag, in Anantnag district. They busied themselves with reaping the benefits of their association with Mirza Afzal Beg, the most powerful minister in the Sheikh government after the 1975 Accord. The members who had been in government service prior to their arrest were reinstated, including Nazir Ahmed Wani and Fazal Haq Qureshi. However, after getting married, Nazir migrated to Saudi Arabia, where he passed away in 2017. Fazal re-joined his service in the secretariat but could not overcome his ideological compulsion. As a result, he was arrested in 1990 allegedly for his association with militants; this was after my retirement from the police service. In fact, before his arrest, he came to me for advice when he was wanted by the police. I advised him to surrender because under the prevailing situation he would have no role to play except on the political front. Accordingly, he was arrested, and after his release, he became an important leader of the Hurriyat Conference, which spearheaded the separatist movement. He visited Pakistan as part of the Hurriyat delegation that met with General Musharraf, the then president of Pakistan, along with other leaders. He was also part of the Hurriyat delegation that met with Prime Minister Vajpayee and Home Minister L.K.

Advani. However, Fazal was later attacked by some unknown gunmen at his Soura residence. This attack may have occurred because he was a member of Hurriyat's moderate faction. Though he survived, he sustained serious injuries, leading to physical disabilities that have significantly impacted his life. Upon their release, the other members of the organization joined various services in the government, banks and other institutions and achieved reasonable success in their lives. Some of them started their own businesses. All the members maintained cordial relations with me, so much so that I was a guest of honour at their weddings.

This is the story of the forgotten guerrillas of Kashmir. Had Al Fatah not been cracked, the insurgency, which the Indian state is still battling in 2023, would have engulfed the state in early 1971, with a stronger and more formidable organizational set-up.

AL FATAH PLAN

According to the blueprint provided by the Pakistani Army, one of the aims and objectives of Al Fatah was the kidnapping and assassination of VIPs and security personnel. In the initial stages, one such assassination was successfully executed when they stabbed and killed Constable Charan Dass. The assassination was considered an important weapon to fight India. Other such assassination plots, which came to light later, were aborted for one reason or the other. On most occasions, the extraordinary vigilance of the state police apparatus saved the situation. The plot to assassinate Prime Minister Indira Gandhi was revealed by none other than Ghulam Rasool Zahgir, the top leader and commander of Al Fatah, during his questioning.

INDIRA GANDHI'S VISIT

During CM Sadiq's regime, Indira Gandhi was scheduled to visit the Valley in September 1966. The Congress government decided to organize a public reception for her; they arranged a procession to bring her from the airport through the busy markets of Srinagar. I was also deputed in plain clothes at Lal Chowk for security. Several meetings were held by the top brass of the police who thoroughly briefed the subordinate officers regarding the smallest details; they had taken cognizance of the added threat perception after the 1965 infiltration. The underground youth groups also posed a substantial threat as they were believed to have obtained some leftover small arms, ammunition and explosives from the retreating Pakistani Mujahideen in 1965. The continued incarceration of Sheikh Mohammad Abdullah, his colleagues and workers posed an additional threat of hostile demonstrations by the general public, particularly the cadres of the PF. The secret agencies of the state even anticipated an attack on the prime minister's motorcade by the angry crowds.

FOOLPROOF SECURITY

The ruling party had arranged for cheering crowds by bringing people from rural areas in specially hired government buses, which made the task more difficult for the police as possible attackers, saboteurs or mischief-mongers could easily mingle with such crowds. To counter any such threat, the police and other security forces were deployed deep into the lanes, by-lanes and interior streets, link roads, etc. along the VVIP route. In view of such a serious threat perception, a multi-tier police deployment was made in the buildings, housetops, shops, restaurants and hotels to completely sanitize the route.

All the places along the route were listed with the names and particulars of the owners, residents, tenants and occupiers of the houses and business establishments. The area between the airport and Nehru Guest House, Chashma Shahi, was divided into zones, sectors and subsectors for the intensive deployment of uniformed and plain-clothes police forces. Gazetted police officers with magistrates were deputed to execute and supervise the security plan in letter and spirit. Special attention was paid to market areas, restaurants and places generally frequented by the public because it was not feasible in those days to completely ban normal public activity or order a lockdown. Areas like Hari Singh High Street, Lal Chowk, Residency Road and Dalgate had large gatherings of Congress party workers and other casual spectators.

Upon arrival, Indira Gandhi boarded an open-hooded car right from the old Srinagar airport (the present airport did not exist) and arrived Nehru Guest House, Chashma Shahi, without any untoward incident. She waved to people lining the streets who seemed relaxed and happy. As the motorcade inched forward, the ruling party workers raised welcome slogans. She arrived at the Nehru Guest House unscathed. However, a couple of years later, in 1972, with Al Fatah unearthed, we got the shock of our lives when Zahgir made a sensational disclosure.

VANTAGE POSITION

'Sir, you know our organization's secret plan envisaged the kidnapping and assassination of VIPs and other pro-India leaders. Mrs Gandhi's public appearance in a procession provided a stellar opportunity for Al Fatah to assassinate her and garner international publicity for our guerrilla war against India. We ensured that the Al Fatah commandos tasked with executing the plan would neither be noticed nor caught. Another associate and I volunteered for this high-profile assassination. After examining the whole route, we selected Shaheen Restaurant situated on the first floor of the arched building at the trisection of the eastern row of buildings along the Hari Singh High Street at the head of the link road leading to Hanuman Mandir. The procession was to pass just in front of Shaheen Restaurant, which had windows facing the main Hari Singh High Street—the VVIP route—as well as towards Hanuman Mandir Link Road. The entry to the stairs leading to the restaurant on the first floor was through Hanuman Mandir Road. Accordingly, the two of us went up to the restaurant before the arrival of Mrs Gandhi's motorcade and occupied a window table a vantage point overlooking Hari Singh High Street. From there, we could easily drop a hand grenade right into her open-hooded car and escape unnoticed through Hanuman Mandir Road. Our window table was hardly about 20 feet above the road. Armed with a couple of hand grenades, we ordered tea and some snacks to justify our presence in the restaurant and also calm our nerves. As soon as we spotted the motorcade taking a right turn at Exhibition Crossing and inching towards Hari Singh High Street, we got ready with our hands on the grenade pins in our pockets. Our heartbeats accelerated as the motorcade slowly moved towards our location.'

LONE CONSTABLE

Zahgir continued his story. 'With the motorcade only about 50 yards away, we pulled ourselves together and prepared to strike. Suddenly, to our utter shock and fear, a Kashmir Police constable in uniform and with a baton in his hand entered the restaurant and sat down, keeping both of us under his gaze. With his sudden appearance, we went into a sort of paralysis. We were so shell-shocked by his mere presence that we could not even breathe properly, let alone make a move. While planning the operation, we had not accounted for such an eventuality; otherwise, we could have arranged for chloroform or ether to knock him unconscious on the spot. Meanwhile, the VVIP motorcade had moved ahead from our vantage point. Perspiring and with fear gripping us, we hurriedly slipped away from the place as we had no alternative but to abandon the plan of assassinating Prime Minister Indira Gandhi.'

Listening to Zahgir, I too was perspiring and wondering how destiny plays a role in saving a human being. This was no less than a miracle. With the deterring presence of a single man in uniform, who neither knew these guys nor had the faintest idea about their dangerous intentions, the assassination plan was thwarted. The khaki had won. Almost two decades later, in 1985, the same khaki cut short the life of the Iron Lady of India.

Chapter 3

Spur of the Moment

This chapter is dedicated to stories of volatile situations, incidents and episodes in the conflict-ridden state, particularly in the Kashmir Valley. Such situations could have engulfed the whole state in a firestorm and resulted in the death of innocent people had we not defused these events with restraint, public relations and out-of-the-box solutions on the spur of the moment. All the stories are related to containing the ever-rising curve of resistance.

NAFIL NAMAZ

To ward off droughts, excessive rains, floods, pandemics and other natural calamities in the Valley, it was customary for Kashmiri Muslims to read the congregational Nafil Namaz on the sprawling Eidgah grounds in Srinagar, seeking forgiveness from Allah to save people from calamities. The holy relics, such as the Alam-e-Sharief (religious standards of historical and spiritual significance), of various holy shrines in Srinagar would also be brought out and displayed at the head of the respective processions proceeding to the venue. All Alam-e-Shariefs would be reverentially kept against the majestic chinar trees on the western side of Eidgah, known as Nafl Bouine (Nafil Chinars). While dispersing after the namaz, two groups, one carrying the Alam-e-Sharief of the Khanqah of Mir Sayyid Ali Hamadani and the other of the shrine of Syed Abdul Rehman, aka Bulbul Shah, would always clash. Both claimed a preferential right to cross a narrow bridge at Braripora on the erstwhile Nallah Mar a canal running through the city that drains the Dal Lake into Anchar Lake and then into Sindh Nallah. Superstitiously, both groups believed that unless the earth was soaked with human blood, their prayers would not be accepted. One or two lives would invariably be lost in such senseless clashes. I had been watching these clashes and bloodshed since my childhood. This local superstition had nothing to do with religion or the namaz read at Eidgah.

BSF FIRING

In 1969, as the Nafil Namaz concluded and the people started to disperse, the two rival groups clashed on the small heritage bridge as usual. The police intervened to separate the groups. Taking advantage of the disturbance, anti-India groups targeted a BSF contingent deployed outside a police post near Tibetan Sarai on the eastern edge of Eidgah. However, these were reserve BSF troops who had not intervened in the scuffle between the rival groups. As stones were being pelted at them, the BSF contingent fired back at the stone-throwing mob, resulting in the death of seven people on the spot. The crowd retrieved the dead bodies and carried them in a procession to Mujahid Manzil near Pathar Masjid—originally the headquarters of the NC and later that of the PF—situated in the thickly populated downtown area on the left bank of the Jhelum and opposite Khanqah-e-Moula. The authorities were worried that the next day, the dead bodies would be carried in a procession to the martyrs' graveyard for burial, potentially leading to more disastrous consequences. Therefore, the administration was faced with a grave issue:

how to retrieve the dead bodies from the politically influential separatist fortress of Mujahid Manzil. Using force was out of question considering the possibility of tragic consequences. Thus, the higher authorities faced a significant law and order challenge.

DATE WITH THE DEAD

As a newcomer to the executive police, neither Eidgah nor Mujahid Manzil fell under my jurisdiction. Both were under the jurisdiction of my colleague and a seasoned police officer, the late Afzal Ahmed, Sub-Divisional Police Officer (SDPO), South City. Nonetheless, DIG Kashmir Peer Ghulam Hassan Shah chose me to retrieve the dead bodies from the formidable fortress of Mujahid Manzil. The plan envisaged by the police hierarchy was to hand the deceased over to their kin for burial on the same night to prevent potential escalation of trouble the next day if they were to be carried in a procession to the martyrs' graveyard. Afzal Ahmed was tasked with contacting the next of kin of the deceased, bringing them on board and ensuring that all arrangements for the funerals were made in advance, with the bodies buried before sunrise. My date with the dead seemed impossible, as any police officer's mere visit to Mujahid Manzil was like walking into enemy territory. I could be attacked and lynched by hostile PF workers who were always present in scores in the lawns. I had only been to the lawns of the place as a schoolgoing kid to hear Sheikh Mohammad Abdullah's speeches.

My personal sources informed me that Mirza Mohammad Afzal Beg was practically putting up there. Therefore, the mission could not be accomplished without Beg's approval. An inexperienced young officer like me was no match for a hardened, wily politician and clever advocate. I had only seen

Mirza Mohammad Afzal Beg during my student days as an important leader speaking on public platforms; I had never met him or spoken to him. This was going to be my maiden one-on-one meeting with him. Before embarking on this mission, I had not even sought an appointment from him for fear of his refusal to meet a junior police officer. Having no alternative, I decided to venture into the possible death trap. I could be mistaken as one of the BSF officers involved in the firing and get lynched, even though I had been neither involved nor present at the scene. Setting my fears aside, I put on a brave face and gathered my courage, determined to execute my Mission Date with the Dead successfully. I reached Mujahid Manzil in the afternoon in a spare truck, accompanied by a few plain-clothes constables to handle and load the dead bodies. I did not carry any weapon with me for self-defence for fear of being misunderstood.

Around a hundred people were sitting on the lawns as I walked past the main gate alone. By the time I was on the tarred driveway, most of the people had gotten up, walked up to me and offered their respectful salaams, much to my surprise. Reciprocating their gesture, I politely responded to their salaams and gave them a smile. Many were known faces. Without engaging in any conversation, I asked them, 'Where is Beg Sahib?' 'Jenab, he is upstairs in his room,' one of them replied. One voluntarily escorted me upstairs to his room. Outside his room, I took a deep breath and gently knocked on the door. 'Come in.' I opened the door slowly, entered the room and offered my salaams. To my pleasant surprise, Beg Sahib respectfully, with a smile, asked me to sit down. Wearing a Kashmiri tweed pheran, he sat on the carpeted floor, correcting some typed letters. As he called for tea, I felt relaxed.

While I was trying to articulate my request for the dead bodies, he asked sarcastically, 'Aap kaise tashreef layein hain?'

(What brings you here?) I introduced myself formally and replied, 'Jenab, main woh lashein lene aaya hoon jo logon ne Eidgah se yahan layi hain.' (Sir, I have come to take the dead bodies that people brought here from Eidgah) 'Unko kal ham khud Mazari Shohda mein tajheez-o-tadfeen karange,' (I personally will bury them in Mazari Shohda tomorrow) he replied firmly. I found myself speaking more confidently than before. I continued, 'Sir, iss se phir bohut khoon kharaba hoga, aur aap bhi shayad logon ko control nahi kar payengey. Aur bohut logon ki jaan bhi ja sakti hai,' firmly cautioning him about the possible escalation of trouble. I thought I had caught him by the horns. Meanwhile, tea was served, and the atmosphere eased. We continued the discussion while having tea.

Ultimately, endorsing my point of view, Beg agreed and permitted me to take the dead bodies. By the time the bodies were loaded into the truck with the help of the policemen and PF workers, it was already dark. However, my joy knew no bounds at the success of my Mission Date with the Dead, especially since I was only at the start of my career. With immense satisfaction, I thought I had won a great battle. I had undoubtedly prevented the further escalation of trouble and possible bloodshed.

The second phase of my mission was to hand over the dead bodies to their kin. This was emotionally tough and dangerous, as the task had to be performed in the dark lanes of the interior city, a volatile and dangerous zone inhabited by anti-India masses. Having come out of Mujahid Manzil unscathed, I was about to walk into another death trap. It was a big gamble because once the families saw the dead bodies of their near and dear ones, they could go out of control and attack me. To my surprise, that operation too was completed very smoothly. In the darkness of night, I handed over the dead bodies to the families of the deceased in their respective homes. I witnessed heart-wrenching scenes of crying mothers, sisters, brothers and old parents wherever I handed over the bodies. Calmly and solemnly, these brave parents and relatives received their dead loved ones with tears in their eyes. It was gratifying to ensure that the last rites were performed before daybreak. Afzal Ahmed, my North Zone counterpart who had prepared the graves, attended to the burial of each one at their respective ancestral graveyards without encountering any trouble. While delivering the dead body of a deaf and dumb young boy from the Renzu family at Anzimar Khanyar, my task was somewhat easier as they were the extended family of Ghulam Rasool Renzu, the ex-speaker of the Legislative Assembly, and friends and in-laws of Abdul Ahad Bhat of Buchwara, my bosom friend who was then an excise and taxation officer. Therefore, the parents of the deceased were extra courteous and thankful to me for bringing the body to their home. I had no difficulty in convincing them to complete all the rites the same night.

As a result of this painful Mission Date with the Dead the previous night, the situation was absolutely normal the next day. An eminent lawyer and friend of mine, Gupte, the then Solicitor General of India, was staying in a houseboat on Dal Lake when he read the news about the firing in a newspaper in the afternoon. He was surprised and could not believe something like that had happened the previous day as life in Srinagar appeared so normal. Nobody could believe that several individuals were killed in BSF firing at Eidgah only the other day. I must salute the statesmanship and humane approach of the late Mirza Mohammad Afzal Beg, who could have chosen to take political advantage of the situation, which could have resulted in a widespread bloodbath of innocent people.

BLASPHEMERS

In 1972, I was faced with a very tough and volatile situation in downtown Srinagar. Mirza Afzal Beg was again destined to come to my rescue in the thick of a highly explosive situation. Beg not only cooperated but also actively helped contain the violent, enraged, frenzied and insensitive mob that was about to lynch a couple of people—the alleged blasphemers. The trouble could have resulted in widespread riots, violence and bloodshed, which could have spilled over to other parts of the state and even to the rest of the country.

On a sunny spring morning, I was at the Rainawari Police Station, Srinagar, for formal inspection. Suddenly, a rumour spread in the city like wildfire that some people had allegedly given a picture of Prophet Muhammad (SAW) to a shopkeeper at Bohri Kadal for framing. Noticing the highly sacrilegious picture, he leaked the information to a few people in the neighbourhood. Within moments, thousands of people had gathered in front of the shop at Bohri Kadal. Upon reaching the scene, I was told that some sensible citizens had rescued the alleged blasphemers from public's wrath and put them up in a nearby house for safety. Otherwise, they would have been lynched even before my arrival. I had no manpower with me except my driver and wireless operator. Though I asked the PCR for some help, the situation deteriorated fast. The three of us positioned ourselves outside the door of the house where the alleged blasphemers were lodged till a few constables arrived from the nearby Maharaj Gunj Police Station. The crowd kept swelling.

Meanwhile, separatist political leaders, including Mirwaiz Moulana Farooq, Mirza Afzal Beg and G.M. Shah, arrived at the spot. The wooden projection of a closed shop was converted into a makeshift platform. One after the other, provocative speeches were delivered against the government and the blasphemers. Mirwaiz demanded their custody and trial by an Islamic court under Islamic jurisprudence. In this situation, my first priority was to rescue the alleged culprits and shift them to the safe custody of a police station. With past experience during Mission Date with the Dead, my only hope was Mirza Afzal Beg. I conceived a plan; slowly tearing through the crowd, I walked alone to speak to him. Unobtrusively, I reached the makeshift platform on the opposite side of the road and whispered to Beg that the first priority of the leaders should be to save the lives of the two people confined in the nearby house. I told him that the crowd was swelling and becoming increasingly out of control and that they might overpower us and lynch us before turning to the accused; I also told him that we might have to fire we fired in self-defence. I requested Beg to keep the people busy with the speeches and help me move the alleged blasphemers to safety. He agreed and asked me to take them away. I made him aware of the danger of attracting the attention of the mob when my jeep started moving to ward the door of the house. The mob was likely to attack us before we could rescue the accused.

I requested him to allow me to use the PF's jeep to give the impression to the mob that the culprits were being handed over to the leaders and not to the police. I convinced him that this was the only way for us to save two precious human lives. I promised him that I would not take them to the police station but to Mujahid Manzil, the PF headquarters. Initially, Beg was reluctant, but with some persuasion, he agreed and asked me to put the culprits in the PF jeep used by G.M. Shah. I went to the door of the house and the party's jeep slowly moved to the door where I was standing, without attracting public attention. The driver was briefed, and the two culprits were brought out of the house. Within a fraction of a second, the jeep was in full view of the mob. Once on the move, the angry crowd attacked the jeep and completely damaged its hood. Yet, the driver accelerated and did not stop till we were at a safe distance and on the way to Mujahid Manzil. The two alleged blasphemers were thus rescued unscathed and locked in a room with a couple of policemen deputed to guard them.

Thereafter, Mirwaiz Moulana Farooq, Mirza Afzal Beg, G.M. Shah and other leaders arrived at Mujahid Manzil with a slogan-shouting, enraged crowd following them in a procession and demanding death for the culprits. Mirwaiz engaged with the crowd and started addressing them, which provided me the golden opportunity to finally save the alleged culprits. After assessing the situation, I requested Beg to allow me to take the culprits to the police station as with crowds swelling by the minute, it was becoming increasingly dangerous to keep them at Mujahid Manzil any longer. Beg understanding the gravity of the situation, kindly agreed. Though the road outside Mujahid Manzil was clear, I did not take them out through the main gate and in full view of the mob gathered in the lawn. The blasphemers were taken out through a small door opening into the back lane of Mujahid Manzil without the crowd noticing us. Meanwhile, the leaders at Mujahid Manzil helped calm the tempers of the mob and assured them that appropriate action would be taken against the culprits. The culprits were safely driven to the police station and subsequently prosecuted under the law.

I must acknowledge the statesmanship of Mirza Afzal Beg. Even though he was spearheading an anti-India movement, he did not politically exploit the situation and nor did he allow others to do so. Mirwaiz Farooq and other leaders, though I did not interact with them directly, also acted like statesmen and cooperated in saving the lives of the accused by calming the tempers of the mob. The situation in which I was was fraught with had multiple dangers and many possible adverse consequences. The blasphemers could have been attacked and killed had I delayed my arrival at the spot. Moreover, had the crowd not been engaged by the separatist leaders at Bohri Kadal, they would have surely razed the house to the ground and attacked the culprits. Using the PF's jeep provided a small window of opportunity to rescue the culprits alive. Using a police jeep would have ended in disaster for all of us. Had the leaders not cooperated, the alleged culprits would have been attacked in Mujahid Manzil itself. The accompanying cops and I would have also been overpowered, and we would have lost our lives as collateral damage.

ANTIBOOZE AGITATION

In 1972, Syed Ali Shah Geelani, a senior hardcore pro-Pakistan leader and member of the J&K Legislative Assembly, launched an agitation demanding a complete ban on the sale and consumption of liquor in Sopore, his home town in north Kashmir. The hidden agenda seemed to be to destabilize the state. Being an emotive issue, even the slightest mishandling by us could have caused the agitation to spread to other cities and major towns in the Valley. The law and order situation was already fragile; one wrong move would infuse it with fresh life and convert it into a full-fledged anti-India political movement with multiple negative dimensions beyond control. Further, the demands were likely to get multiplied with each passing day. It was a subtle political move to arouse the people's religious feelings to disturb peace across the troubled Valley. I gave a thought to the serious problem at hand and chalked out an innovative strategy to deal with the agitation. Peer Ghulam Hassan Shah, DIG Kashmir Range, and Hamidullah Khan, the DC, were on board.

I met with all the influential people of the town to gauge their feelings about Geelani's move. All of them unequivocally supported the agitation, irrespective of religious beliefs and political affiliations. As it was unwise to swim against the tide, I sprung a surprise when I declared my support for the demand and asked the officer in charge of the government wine shop to wind up. He was naturally reluctant to do so in the absence of the approval of his higher authorities. In a swift tactical move, I locked the shop. In general, people welcomed my move to close down the shop. The sting was taken off Geelani's agitation, with the situation being contained and not allowed to snowball.

Sopore, being a very sensitive and volatile town in north Kashmir, was substantially under the influence of Geelani's Jamaat-e-Islami (JI); consequently, it could go up in flames if the situation was allowed to escalate. However, my actions drew criticism from the official hierarchy of the state excise department, including the minister in charge, who viewed my intervention as high-handed. They complained to the chief minister about my actions. I had already taken my DIG Range on board, who may have briefed CM Sayed Mir Qasim, and that is why the government did not interfere.

For Geelani, my action was unexpected. He was left with no issue to agitate as there were no other liquor outlets in town. Suddenly, to infuse fresh blood into his agitation, he raised the level of his demand to a statewide ban on liquor. With local support dwindling, he decided to escalate his agitation by courting arrest along with other JI cadres. On the scheduled date and time, I personally camped at the Sopore Police Station and issued instructions not to stop the demonstrators anywhere in the town, provided they remained peaceful. With Syed Ali Shah Geelani at the lead, the slogan-shouting procession started marching peacefully towards the police station. When they were about to reach the police station, I came out and stood at the gate, along with some of my local officers, blocking their entry. The procession stopped at the gate and Geelani approached me, saying, 'Main aur mere saathi giriftari dene aaye hain' (My colleagues and I have come to be arrested). I refused: 'Why should I arrest you and the others? You have not committed any crime.' I continued, within everyone's earshot, 'We can't arrest people as and when they choose to court arrest without any legitimate reason. No law permits me to arrest you at your request. Sir, this is a police station, not a rest house'—I stood stern and serious.

With my unexpected move, Geelani was left flabbergasted. He could not think of what to do next. He was faced with an unexpected situation beyond his imagination. He toned down and, in a friendly manner, he whispered to me to allow him to court arrest. 'Sorry, it will not be possible for me to "accommodate" you,' I told him firmly. He did not know what to do. His supporters were also confused. However, after some more haggling, I devised an out-of-the-box compromise to 'accommodate' him. I quietly whispered to him to stage a sit-in on the main road in front of the police station and symbolically stop traffic for a few seconds. Thereafter, he could come and court arrest. He and his supporters did exactly what I suggested. They stopped a state road transport corporation bus on its way from Bandipore to Sopore for a few seconds. Thereafter, Geelani and a couple of his supporters came to the police station gate. Only he was permitted to enter and court arrest. The rest of the crowd continued peacefully shouting slogans outside. Geelani was offered a cup of tea while we discussed his agitation. I advised him to call it off in view of our accepting his local demand. 'Pushing this agenda further is meaningless; it will not bear any fruitful result,' I told him. He discussed other matters pertaining to his constituency. Satisfied with my assurance, he left the police station and addressed his followers outside. The crowd dispersed peacefully with no ill will towards the police. He did not pursue the agitation further, and normalcy returned to Sopore.

After a few months, taking advantage of the closure of government liquor shops, some antisocial elements in Sopore took up the clandestine trade of liquor smuggling, which went on under the very nose of those who were agitating for the ban. This encouraged the excise department authorities to reopen the liquor shop. That is exactly what I had thought would happen.

CUSTODIAL DEATH

In 1975, Hindal Haidar Tyabji was the DC of Anantnag. We had cordial working relations. This huge district, which covered all of south Kashmir, from Jawahar Tunnel to Sempora, Pampore, was managed and administered bi him efficiently. Hindal, a gentleman par excellence, belonged to a bureaucratic and nationalist family. His mother is credited with designing the national flag of the country after Independence.

One morning, I received an SOS wireless message from a police station in Shopian about the death of an accused in police custody. Given the volatile nature of Shopian, a town in south Kashmir, all the local shops and business establishments instantly closed down in protest against the alleged custodial death. Assessing the sensitivity of the situation, particularly the aggressive nature of the residents, I informed the DC and requested him to get ready so that we could immediately leave for Shopian before the situation was exploited by antisocial and anti-India elements. Travelling together at top speed, with me behind the wheel of my official jeep, we reached Shopian and saw the whole town in a state of lockdown. Protesters had converged in front of the Jamia Masjid in the middle of town. Cutting through the crowd, I drove straight to the police station. No one in the crowd made any attempt to stop our vehicle or get violent. At the police station, Head Constable Mohrir was the seniormost official present as the SHO was on leave and the second officer had gone to a remote area to investigate a private complaint under section 107 of the CrPC, a petty matter, which was just a device to justify police intervention in private matters for ulterior motives.

According to the head constable, the deceased, a habitual cattle lifter and burglar, was the son-in-law of a notorious cattle lifter of the area—Ahad Goru. A Bad Character number 10 (BC No. 10), Goru was an inter-district and intra-district cattle lifter and headed a network of cattle lifters. Goru's name featured in Register No. 10 of the police station, and his movements were restricted under the provisions of the Bad Characters Surveillance Act. The police were supposed to make frequent domestic visits to him to ensure his presence. Any deviation would entail prosecution under section 188 of the Ranbir Penal Code, but all this was only on paper. He would get 'rasoom', which is a sort of protection money, from the villagers of the area in cash and kind. In the event of any cattle-lifting incident in his area, Ahad Goru would be responsible for tracing the stolen cattle and restoring them to the lawful owners against additional payment to be shared with the actual cattle lifter. This business was conducted with the knowledge of the local police who allegedly got their share of the unlawful activities.

The victim, Goru's son-in-law, had been deputizing on his behalf. He had gone to an adjacent village to settle a deal with a party whose livestock had been stolen. While discussions were going on, the tempers of the other party suddenly ran high, resulting in a scuffle wherein serious injuries were caused to Goru's son-in-law. The party responsible for causing the injuries to the deceased, realizing the possibility of getting arrested for assaulting him, planted a few household items on his person, tied him up with ropes and falsely accused him of trespassing to commit burglary. The deceased was taken to the police station by his assailants and a report was lodged against him. The assistant sub-inspector (ASI), who was in charge of the police station at that point of time, registered a case of burglary and theft against the injured without taking any cognizance of the injuries on his person. Moreover, he did not bother to refer him to a hospital for treatment. The injured accused was formally arrested and locked up. The ASI left for a 'bahak' (the grazing area of Gujjars and Bakarwals), a faraway area not connected by road.

Unfortunately, Goru's son-in-law's condition deteriorated and Head Constable Mohrir carried him to a nearby hospital, where the doctors referred him to SMHS Hospital, Srinagar, due to his critical condition. Mohrir arranged for a taxi in which he carried the injured accused, but he died en route to Srinagar. Mohrir brought his dead body back to the police station. In the morning, as soon as the people found out about the custodial death, they called for a shutdown. Though every human life is precious, one can't imagine a shutdown in sympathy for a habitual criminal and extorter. The incident was exploited by anti-India forces to disturb the peace on the pretext of custodial killing.

After acquainting with the actual facts, I chalked out a line of action to pacify the agitating public. Mohrir and I reached Jamia Masjid where people had assembled outside. We climbed up to the verandah of the mosque and requested the people, who were raising provocative slogans, to calm down. Some respected individuals and ringleaders, whom I knew, were heard asking the people to sit down: 'Let's hear out Watali.' Amid the chanting of slogans, they sat down. While addressing the crowd, I expressed my grief regarding the sad and unfortunate death of the person in police custody. Without getting into the specifics of the case,

I announced the action taken in the matter. I told them, 'I have suspended the ASI for negligence as he failed to take cognizance of the multiple injuries on the person of the deceased and also for his failure to send him to a hospital for treatment.' Continuing my address, I declared, 'I have ordered the registration of a murder case against the individuals responsible for allegedly beating the deceased mercilessly and causing grievous injuries to him, which resulted in his death.' My announcement had a magical effect as the crowd responded with cheers. I assured them that the person responsible for the murder would not be spared and all culprits would be brought to justice. At my request, the DC announced ex gratia cash relief for the dependants of the deceased. As soon as we concluded, the situation defused; the shutdown was called off, and normalcy was restored. We stayed with the crowd for some time to chit-chat in a friendly atmosphere and later held a meeting with the esteemed individuals of the area at the police station regarding this case and other community issues. The SHO, who was on leave, was recalled immediately and entrusted with the investigation. With a speedy investigation, the accused individuals, against whom a prima face case was established, were arrested. They were tried, convicted and sentenced by the court. The ASI was given a severe departmental punishment for gross negligence and carelessness in discharging his duties. Notwithstanding the political motive of some elements, people in general responded positively and a volatile situation was defused.

This was our urgent response to the problem. Through the long-term investment of goodwill with the public, we were able to defuse the situation. The trust and confidence built between the people and police is key to better administration. The mantra was to quickly respond to and address people's grievances and establish a working relation with influential citizens so that they can help whenever the police are faced with such difficult situations.

MURTI AND MOSQUE

I would now like to share an explosive incident from 1981. A project to widen the internal roads of downtown Srinagar necessitated the removal of some chronic bottlenecks caused by old residential buildings, shrines, mosques, etc. People did not resist the removing and relocating of their houses or places of worship after due compensation was paid by the state.

While I was attending to my normal office work, I got a call from a highly respected person and Islamic scholar, the late Mufti Jalal-ud-Din, one of the Grand Muftis of the state who was also a frontline veteran freedom fighter. Mufti informed me that while digging the foundation of a demolished mosque in downtown Srinagar, the labourers had retrieved a huge murti (idol). Mufti asked for my advice. Before replying to him, the possible consequences flashed through my mind. I did not have many options, I thought. The murti's discovery, if made public, would result in a huge controversy between the two communities; moreover, it could give rise to communal tension as well as riots, although Kashmir had no such past history. This episode, if not handled prudently and swiftly, was also likely to give rise to resistance forces.

Therefore, I made up my mind about the action to be taken while Mufti sahib was still on the line. I requested him, 'Sir, make sure that the labourers cover the murti with earth till I do something and call you back. Until then, the matter is strictly between you and me.' I further insisted, 'Please take care to conceal the murti from public view.' Given that the site was on a busy thoroughfare, I asked an officer of Srinagar District Police Lines to send a section of constables in civvies to the spot with a truck and wait for further instructions; I did not tell him anything about the task ahead. Simultaneously, I rang up the

SHO of the concerned police station and instructed him to rush to the spot where a police contingent would be arriving shortly with a truck. I further instructed the SHO to remove the murti swiftly, ensure that it was covered with earth and transport it to the police station without delay. Concurrently, I also contacted a senior officer of the Archaeological Survey of India and asked him to depute his representative to the police station to collect a rare murti that could be added to their collection. I did not disclose to him the location from where the murti had been obtained.

Everyone efficiently performed their duties and strictly in accordance with the roles assigned to each one of them. I did not even have to leave my office. The murti was removed without the passers-by or neighbouring shopkeepers finding out about it. At the police station, it was handed over to the officer deputed by the Archaeological Survey of India, who carried it in the same truck without unloading, as advised in advance. With our quick response, we were able to prevent a possible communal situation in an already conflict-ridden state, which could have escalated into prolonged conflict between the two communities. It could have also disturbed the age-old peaceful relations between them. With the timely information received from Mufti sahib and the quick response of the police, the spirit of Kashmiriyat was preserved.

Believe me, I had not even informed my senior officers till the murti was finally deposited in the stores of the Archaeological Survey of India. They were very happy, and later, the DGP informed the CM, who conveyed his appreciation to me and my whole team. Though we did not have very powerful electronic media in those days, a vibrant print media did exist in the Valley. In view of the swift and discreet handling, they did not discover these developments. The general public will come to know about the incident through this book.

TOMBSTONE

Notwithstanding the rich heritage of intercommunity brotherhood in Kashmir, there were always elements, particularly among the youth, who were always on the lookout for sensitive issues to pursue their agenda. Sometimes, unscrupulous and selfish individuals in society do not hesitate to create a situation that can turn into a full-fledged firestorm, just for their political aggrandizement and to satisfy their own vested interests.

In 1981, I was faced with one such situation in Srinagar. On the Hazuri Bagh (presently Iqbal Park) side of Gonikhan in the Maharaja Bazar locality of Srinagar, a Hindu temple has existed since times immemorial. It is managed by the Sanatan Dharam Sabha, a local socioreligious organization of Punjabi Hindus who have been living in the Valley for more than a century. On one side of the temple, facing the eastern side of Iqbal Park, there existed an old and dilapidated four-storey wooden building, which was the property of the temple. One evening, I got a phone call from Lala Dharamvir Batra—a prominent businessman, an oil king of the state and the head of the Sabha—asking for an appointment. Their delegation wanted to see me urgently because there was a likelihood of a grave clash between two communities. Although I had no official intelligence from any agency about such a possibility, I asked them to come to my official residence at once.

Batra, accompanied by a few other respectable Punjabi Hindu businessmen whom I knew very well, came to my residence at Jawahar Nagar. Batra told me that the Sabha had planned to construct a multi-storey shopping complex after demolishing the dilapidated building, which had been declared dangerous by the municipal authorities. The Sabha had already obtained the necessary permissions. Accordingly, they had demolished the old structure and had started excavating the foundation for the new building. That same evening, after the work had stopped for the night, a group of people from the local Muslim community came and raised a green flag on the excavated site, claiming the place to be a graveyard. According to Batra, they further claimed that the grave of a Mughal prince, who had died in the Valley 600 years ago as indicated by the engraved date on the tombstone, lay there. They also propagated that the prince was a pious saint, and therefore, it was a holy site for the Muslims. A reasonably large crowd of men, women and children had already collected there, and Kashmiri sweet tea (kehwa) was being served to all who were raising religious slogans. This whole situation had developed only an hour or so before they had called me. Batra informed me that some of the youth from their community were ready go to the spot to retrieve the site using force, but they were dissuaded by their elders who feared a clash. Furthermore, Batra explained that neither their staff nor the labourers had noticed any tombstone at the place while digging the foundation.

At that particular time, while the delegation was with me, the site had already been converted into a Muslim shrine for all practical purposes. A potentially dangerous situation stared me in the face. Over time, Lalaji (Batra) and other members of the community had developed a lot of faith in me. 'Please allow me to handle the matter in my own way.' I assured them that I would restore the site to them, provided their claim was genuine. I also advised them to not visit the spot, emphasizing that none of their community members, particularly the youth, should go there without my permission. They assured me of all cooperation and left me to deal with the explosive situation.

I mulled over the issue in my mind with all its possible outcomes. The situation demanded immediate and decisive action as any delay could be fatal. I decided to act the same night because by the next day, the situation was likely to go out of control with more and more crowd from other parts of the city expected to arrive at the place. The anti-India political faction was also likely to exploit the already explosive situation. Any dithering to take decisive action was likely to escalate the issue into a conflict with the potential to claim innocent lives. That night was the only time available to us. I left my residence and called a meeting of the concerned officers at the Shergarhi Police Station and requisitioned additional manpower from the PCR. Selecting a group of proficient police officers to assist me in Mission Tombstone, we marched to the site to demonstrate our will to act firmly.

Once at the site, we used the public address system to announce a curfew in the area. All the people near the site were directed to disperse and return to their homes. With this announcement, most of the crowd hurriedly dispersed. A few of them, who belonged to a family surnamed 'Mogul', continued to defiantly occupy the place. However, we swiftly took action and arrested all of them, except the women and children who were ushered into the lane leading to their houses. The tombstone, along with the religious flag that had been hoisted, was removed and transported to the police station. An armed police guard was stationed at the so-called Mogul graveyard site and no one was allowed access within an area of 250 yards around the site. The night passed peacefully as we had imposed restrictions on the movement of the people living in the adjacent areas of Goni Khan and Maharaja Bazar. Free movement was allowed in the rest of the area. Prima facie, it appeared that a few members of the local Mogul family, living nearby in the interiors of Maharaj Bazar, had concocted this covert plan to grab the prime commercial site.

After clearing the area, I examined the tombstone at the police station and observed the engravings very closely, which revealed some faint marks of possibly erased engravings that were not decipherable to the naked eye. The tombstone was, therefore, referred to the Forensic Science Laboratory for examination to decipher any hidden engravings, if present. We contacted some respected residents of the locality who had suspected the involvement of a particular family in orchestrating the scheme to grab the plot of land by exploiting the religious sentiments of the gullible people, particularly the youth. On the assurance given by these respected individuals, we gradually lifted the restrictions during the day, and by evening, normalcy had been restored, in less than 24 hours. As a result of timely police intervention, the accused persons who had been arrested were isolated as they did not get support from any quarter.

At our request, the laboratory gave an interim report, supported by photographs of hidden engravings. Their report disclosed that the original engravings on the tombstone, which had been erased, were hardly a year old. The erased engravings could be clearly discernible in the photographs and the deceased's name and date of death were clearly legible. The purported sixth-century engravings proved to be recent. On the basis of this disclosure, the arrested individuals were thoroughly questioned. They admitted to conceiving this dangerously covert plan to grab the prime land. They also admitted to stealing the tombstone from the Malateng graveyard situated in the foothills of Shankaracharya hill. They further admitted that the existing engravings were erased with the help of an expert tombstone maker, who engraved sixteenth-century dates on it, superimposing the erased ones. It was conclusively established that the alleged sixteenth-century engravings were recently carved on the stolen tombstone and installed at the site.

A criminal conspiracy had been hatched by the deceitful members of the family to grab the site. Their act would have surely led to bloody consequences had we not acted fast. Additionally, there was a grave possibility of the anti-India youth exploiting the situation, potentially leading to bloodshed. Despite all overt and covert provocations and pressures, by remaining aloof from this affair and by supporting the claim of the Punjabi Hindus, the public in general upheld the noble principles of Kashmiriyat that flows in their blood. Owned by the Sanatan Dharam Sabha, a beautiful multilevel shopping complex exists at the site, today which is occupied by tenants from all communities, mostly Muslims.

SEPARATIST PLATFORM

Upon the removal of the Farooq government by Governor Jagmohan and the swearing in of a defectors' ministry, the people had lost faith in Indian democracy. It was a major blunder that ultimately led to the alienation of the youth, and later, to militancy. However, after the assassination of Mrs Gandhi and Rajiv Gandhi becoming the prime minister, governor's rule was imposed in the state on 7 March 1986, dissolving the defectors' government. During the first phase of Governor Jagmohan's term, he ordered a ban on the slaughter of sheep on the occasion of Janmashtami, (a pre-1947 practice under the Maharaja's rule). This decision thrust Qazi Nisar, an Islamic scholar and Mirwaiz of south Kashmir, into the political arena in a big way. Openly defying the ban, he slaughtered several sheep at Lal Chowk in Anantnag. Qazi carved out an appropriate political and ecclesiastical space for himself and constantly raised different issues, including challenging the validity of the accession of the state. Subsequently, he contested the assembly elections in 1987 under the banner of the Muslim United Front (MUF), but lost, allegedly due to rigging.

He grabbed one such opportunity to assert his separatist and rebel leadership when a law and order situation emerged as a result of the death of a youth during the investigation of a case pertaining to the elopement (alleged kidnapping) of a young Kashmiri Pandit girl from Kulgam with her Muslim boyfriend. Though both were legally adults, the police had registered a case based on the complaint of the girl's parents. Even such cases were registered suo moto by the police. The couple had vanished into thin air, and the girl's parents had moved the J&K High Court. I was summoned and admonished by the high court for our failure to recover the girl. This resulted in intensified efforts by the police to recover the girl. Although numerous places were raided within and outside the state, the eloped couple could not be traced.

This case, however, neither attracted any public attention from the Pandit community nor did it assume any communal colour. Unfortunately, the situation took an ugly turn when the suspect's cousin, summoned for questioning by the police, while being transported in a police truck from Anantnag to Kulgam, suddenly jumped into the ferocious Veshaw Nallah from the Khudwani bridge and disappeared into the water.

Javed Makhdoomi, SSP, Anantnag, informed me about this incident around sunset. He told me that the people were extremely worked up, with tempers running very high. All the people of the area in and around Khudwani were out on the streets to protest the alleged custodial death of the youth. Realizing the possible repercussions and potential exploitation of the issue by secessionists the next day, I instructed the SSP to get the body of the boy out the same night; otherwise, the police would be accused of murder, and there would be widespread violence spilling over to the entire Valley. I informed Governor Jagmohan about the tragic incident the same evening. Thanks to the district police, their night-long efforts bore the desired results, and the body was recovered the same night. I directed the SSP to hand over the body to the relatives after a post-mortem and ensure that the last rites were completed before sunrise the next morning for fear of attempts by politicians to politicize the issue. The SSP acted accordingly, and the next morning, everything was normal all around. Throughout the night, I was in contact with Governor Jagmohan to keep him updated about the situation.

The next morning, I decided to visit the bereaved family in Frisal village (a JI stronghold) to offer my condolences and to assure them of suitable action against any person found responsible for negligence. I sought the governor's permission to announce some relief for the family. He appreciated the idea and told me to go ahead and announce whatever I deemed proper. As I reached Anantnag, I found Deputy Commissioner Swami Raj and SSP Javed Makhdoomi huddled together waiting for me. To my surprise, both were unanimously against visiting the village. They informed me that at that point in time, a public meeting convened by Qazi Nisar and some other separatist/religious leaders was in progress and tempers were running high. They running of the view that our visit might provoke them and aggravate an already volatile situation. Considering their suggestion regarding the possible fallout, I told them that we were not going there for any purpose other than to offer our condolences and to help the family in their time of extreme grief. 'Our conscience is clear; you have not killed the boy. He committed suicide in full public view. No matter what happens, we must go. In our absence, political leaders are likely to further provoke the villagers in an attempt to widen the area of trouble and convert it into a Valley-wide agitation,' I explained to them. 'If we go there, we will be catching the bull by the horn.' Both of them were convinced, and we left for the village without any additional manpower accompanying us. The SHO of the area and a few constables of the concerned police station were reportedly patrolling the village, without arms, in view of the ongoing public meeting.

As soon as we reached Frisal, we came across the public meeting, with leaders speaking from a raised platform erected in an open space in front of the deceased's house. There were approximately a few hundred villagers in attendance. After assessing the situation in a fraction of a second and identifying all the leaders on the dais, I made up my mind about our next move. It was not an easy task! What mattered at that time was the goodwill cultivated by a police officer through consistent public engagement and pro-people policies. I had the advantage of having served in the district as SSP for about five years. I was very well known to the villagers and the elders. I had to grab the initiative without backing down. With all these positive thoughts flashing through my mind, I decided to proceed towards the platform. 'Follow me, please,' I whispered to the DC and SSP. Slowly, the three of us started walking towards the platform without disturbing the audience.

As soon as Qazi Nisar, who was on the mic, noticed us, he became more aggressive in his address. Calmly, I ascended the platform from behind with the DC and SSP in tow. As we sat down on the rug-covered platform, we greeted all of the leaders and shook hands. Everyone, including Qazi, was very well known to me from when I was posted in Anantnag. I sat next to Moulvi Ghulam Rasool Qadri of Jammeeyat-i-Ahlihadees, a well-known moderate scholar with whom I had a great equation from my days in Anantnag. 'I don't understand why the police interfere when a boy and a girl, who are adults, get married,' thundered Qazi, indirectly referring to the elopement of the Muslim boy and Pandit girl. 'This amounts to undue interference in the people's personal lives. I warn the police that they should change their attitude,' Qazi warned us in no uncertain terms. Taking mental note of his declaration, I decided to teach him a lesson and beat him at his own game. I made up my mind on how to defuse the explosive situation and turn it in our favour. 'Qazi sahib has fallen in his own trap,' I whispered to Ghulam Rasool Qadri, advising him to be cautious in his speech. Qazi finished and sat down next to me. We exchanged customary salaams. Qadri rose to speak. His speech was had no provocation. After he finished, there was no other speaker, so I quickly got up and grabbed the mic to speak uninvited. I started with the Darood-u-Salaam and said, 'With the permission of the organizers of this public meeting, I would like to say a few words.' None of the leaders or anyone in the audience objected or adversely reacted to my suo moto address even though I was dressed in uniform.

Addressing the gathering, I expressed my extreme sorrow and grief over the unfortunate and tragic death of the youth. There was pin drop silence. After offering my condolences and sympathies to the bereaved family, I announced an inquiry into the facts and circumstances that had led to the youth's demise. I continued, 'In case any police official is found to be directly or indirectly responsible for the death of the youth, he will be punished under the law and sent to jail. If the death has been caused due to the negligence of any police official, he too will be punished and dismissed from service. Pending inquiry, the policemen escorting the deceased have been suspended and their uniforms stripped.' Though the audience was listening patiently, I could not feel any change in their mood. I further announced, 'Governor sahib has approved the appointment of one person of the bereaved family to the Public Health Engineering Department in place of the deceased, who was working as a class four employee.' With this announcement, the audience seemed to relax. I also announced a grant of five thousand rupees to be paid to the bereaved family to meet the expenses of his last rites.

Feeling the change in the audience's mood, I assumed a serious tone and raised my voice a bit, saying, 'Please listen carefully to what I am going to tell you now. Qazi Nisar sahib, who is the Mirwaiz of south Kashmir and a scholar of Islamic law, has just issued a fatwa from this very platform. The fatwa states that if a boy and a girl, who are adults, marry each other even without their parents' consent, the police have no power to interfere. This fatwa is binding on us as well as on you as parents. Therefore, from this day onwards, nobody should report such matters to the police because in view of the fatwa, we cannot take any action.' Elaborating further, I gave some hypothetical examples, 'If, God forbid, one of your daughters elope and marry a boy of her choice without your knowledge or permission, please don't bother to report the incident to the police.' I continued, hammering the point further, much to the Qazi's embarrassment. By then, the crowd was getting restless. Abruptly, one elderly person got up and shouted, 'Jenab, what are you saying? Do you expect us to watch silently while our daughters elope with their boyfriends?' 'This is the fatwa Qazi sahib has announced from this platform. You and I are bound by that,' I told the old man, expressing my helplessness.

Qazi, already nervous, grasped the gravity of the situation that was developing against him. I had struck a nerve. He whispered to me, 'Jenab, yeh aap kya kah rahe hain?' (Jenab, what are you saying?) I did not take note of what he was saying and continued to exploit the moment to dismantle his authority, till there was a commotion. My speech had the desired effect. The whole crowd suddenly rose to their feet and shouted slogans against Qazi. I appealed to the audience to sit down and listen to me. Once they calmed down, I continued, 'I am a Kashmiri by birth, and I am aware of local sensitivities. We are a tight-knit society. I know how parents and other members of the family suffer indignation and social stigmatization when an unmarried girl elopes with her boyfriend. It amounts to the social death of all family members. Here, from this platform, I assure you that the police are always with you and at your service, notwithstanding what Qazi sahib has said.' People again shouted anti-Qazi slogans with more intensity. The leaders sitting on the platform got up to leave. Qazi nervously asked me, 'What have you done? You have put my life in danger.' By now, there was complete pandemonium with nonstop slogan-shouting against Qazi. 'Don't worry, I am here. I will protect you and ensure your safe passage,' I assured Qazi. Catching his arm, I pulled him away from the crowded platform and pushed him into my car without his chappals, which he couldn't find. Seated in my car, I advised him calmly, 'Qazi sahib, you must always take care of the local sensibilities before commenting on sensitive issues regarding our women and girls. Place yourself in the position of their parents.' In this manner, a potentially adverse situation emanating from a separatist platform was converted into a favourable one. This was possible only because of our long-standing investment in goodwill in the area over the years. Despite their being hardcore supporters of the JI, a pro-Pakistan outfit, they had pretty good working relations and regard for me.

With Qazi sahib having passed away, I should not have narrated this story, but I thought it was an important incident for future historians to record. I have always held Qazi Nisar in high esteem. His father, Qazi Ghulam Mohammad, a highly revered religious personality of the area, was also very well known to me. Qazi was subsequently gunned down by militants, depriving Kashmir of his valuable services and leadership. His martyrdom changed the landscape of militancy, provoking anti-Pakistan demonstrations in Anantnag for the first time.

Decades later, in 2010, some elderly residents of the village mentioned this incident to my son Shafqat, who was DIG, South Kashmir Range, and had visited the same village to look into some alleged excesses by central security forces personnel during the 2010 uprising.

BATTLE OF WITS

Holidaying on a weekend, I was with my family at Pahalgam as everything was normal in the district. On Monday, when we were due to return, my children insisted on staying for one more day and forced me to be with them. Succumbing to their pressure, I decided to stay; normally, such occasions of being with my family were rare due to my busy daily schedule. Almost simultaneously, the SHO of Anantnag, Ghulam Mohammad Paul, called me to inform that all the shops in the town had suddenly closed for unknown reasons, though they normally opened in the morning. Suspecting that violence was about to erupt, I decided to leave; my plans to spend another day with my family did not materialize. I left immediately as a delay in my arrival could worsen the situation. Driving as fast as I could, I wondered why there would be a shutdown in the town when everything appeared normal in other parts of the Valley. There was no contentious issue either to justify a protest. Moreover, no individual or party had given an open call for a shutdown. I kept analysing the situation in my mind. Provisionally, I concluded that closure of shops might be the handiwork of some underground youth resistance outfit through a whisper campaign to disturb normalcy, with the aim of engaging the police in a battle of stone pelting, which could worsen the situation and lead to firing. By the process of elimination, I zeroed in on a young man who could have been the brain behind this snap call or who could at least throw some light on the issue.

Nearing Aishmuqam, I sent a wireless message to the SHO to pick up Qasim Sajad, a local bookseller who had his shop near Rehat Dedi Masjid on Lal Chowk. Though ostensibly he was not very politically active, he was well connected and always aware of the covert activities of underground groups. As I was approaching Mattan, a tehsil, the SHO called back to report that when he picked up Qasim Sajad, all the shops immediately opened. His very presence in the police station had a magical effect, I thought. I had hit the bullseye. I drove straight to the police station where I met Qasim Sajad and exchanged some pleasantries with him without giving him any impression about my suspicion of his involvement. Feigning ignorance regarding the whole affair, I asked him why he had come to the police station. He was silent. I changed the topic and spoke to him about other things. To keep him guessing, I pretended to admonish the SHO for unnecessarily bringing him to the police station. The circumstances indicated that he was somehow connected with someone responsible for the shutdown. I had my finger right on the pulse. It was nothing but a battle of wits.

I maintained friendly relations with him until his passing a few years later. I can't forget the contents of a letter he wrote to me after the 1977 elections, when I was given a punishment posting to the Police Training School, Udhampur. Qasim Sajad's letter began with a couplet by the famous poet Faiz Ahmad Faiz, which I reproduce here to give the readers an idea of the nature of our relationship:

Kar raha tha gham-e-jahan ka hisaab,
aaj tum yaad behisaab aaye.

(I was pondering over my past sorrows,
And missed you a lot.)

SHEIKH LEADS EID PRAYERS

Srinagar's Eidgah, situated on the western end of the city, holds historic significance. It is well known that the land was purchased for this purpose over 600 years ago by the Central Asian Saint Hazrat Amir-e-Kabir, Mir Syed Ali Hamadani (RA), and dedicated to the Muslim community. I remember that as a child, I would accompany my grandfather, father and uncle to Eidgah on every Eid for namaz. Before militancy engulfed the state, the congregational Eid prayers were offered by about one lakh people twice a year. However, no congregational Eid namaz has been held there in many years.

Earlier, due to political differences, Eid prayers were offered separately by the supporters of Mirwaiz Moulvi Yusuf Shah and Mirwaiz Moulvi Ghulam Nabi Hamdani. The former group consisted of supporters of the Muslim Conference (Bakras), whereas the latter were supporters of the NC (Shers). There used to be frequent clashes between the two groups even on Eid. Mirwaiz Moulvi Yusuf Shah would deliver the religious sermon at Aali Masjid on the northern end of Eidgah, whereas Mirwaiz Hamadani would address his followers in the main Eidgah ground, the namaz venue.

The management and upkeep of Eidgah was the responsibility of the Muslim Auqaf Trust, headed by Sheikh Mohammad Abdullah. It was later taken over by the Mufti Mohammad Sayeed government and renamed the Muslim Waqf Board, a government entity. Due to the unnecessary staff appointed by the Board, it was not possible to take up any development programmes. The entire income from devotees' offerings was consumed by the staff, leading to a great setback for a once viable and well-managed trust. After the abrogation of Article 370 of the Indian Constitution, the Central Waqf Act was applied to the state, but the consequences remain to be seen.

Traditionally, at Eidgah, Eid prayers were led by the hereditary Imam-e-Hai. In 1975, when Sheikh sahib assumed power, he ensured that both rival parties—Sher and Bakra—offered Eid prayers jointly at Eidgah as a gesture of unity. This demonstration of unity between the two rival groups was welcomed by the people in general and the supporters of both parties in particular. Imam-e-Hai, who was of quite an advanced age, passed away in 1981. His son, who was his natural successor, did not choose to accept this ecclesiastical position, as he was a very senior officer of the Audit and Accountants Services of the GoI. Reportedly, despite persuasion by many respected elders, including the Auqaf trustees, he relinquished his position as the head. This created an awkward situation on the occasion of Eid-ul-Azha, as there was no authorized person to lead the namaz. The Auqaf Trust had advertised the position but was yet to appoint an eligible person. The consequences of this situation had not been assessed in advance by either the Auqaf or the government.

At the time fixed for prayer, Maulvi Farooq also joined. Mirwaiz Farooq and Sheikh Mohammad Abdullah stood in the front row. I also joined, though I was on duty and in my uniform. Suddenly, Maulvi Mohammad Yusuf, aka Peer Manki, appeared on the minmber (the place in front from where the Imam leads the prayer) to lead the prayer and loudly gave a call: Allah-u-Akbar. The audience, including Sheikh sahib, responded and followed the call. However, Mirwaiz Farooq lunged to the minmber and pulled Peer Manki out and forcibly disengaged Sheikh's arms folded in namaz. 'We do not accept Peer Manki as Imam-e-Hai as he is your partyman,' Mirwaiz shouted at Sheikh. The devotees throughout Eidgah turned panicky as the drama was audible through the public address system. Watching the whole scene, I feared a serious clash and large-scale disturbances on the auspicious occasion. It would be a disaster, I thought. A stampede could cost numerous lives, including those of women and children. Sheikh, however, coolly but firmly retorted, 'What can we do now at such short notice?' Mirwaiz Farooq rose to the occasion by displaying his extraordinary statesmanship when at the height of the tension, he asked Sheikh sahib, 'You lead the prayers. We will follow you.' Sheikh hesitated, but Mirwaiz held him by his left arm and led him towards the minmber. I also followed holding Sheikh's right arm, not believing my eyes and ears.

Sheikh called 'Allah-u-Akbar', and the devotees, more than a lakh in number, responded with 'Allah-u-Akbar' and folded their arms. The prayers concluded in a few minutes, and people rushed to congratulate Sheikh as well as Mirwaiz. The people's joy knew no bounds as such a huge congregation had for the first time offered namaz, with Sheikh Mohammad Abdullah as the Imam. It was truly a historic occasion. The people dispersed peacefully shouting pro-Sheikh and pro-Mirwaiz slogans. On that day, a message was sent across loud and clear that Sheikh Mohammad Abdullah was the undisputed leader of the masses.

I felt highly relieved and elated as an imminent catastrophe was avoided, which could have caused the loss of many lives on such an auspicious day. It happened only because of the statesmanship of Mirwaiz Farooq and the unparalleled popularity of Sheikh Mohammad Abdullah. Mirwaiz Maulvi Mohammad Farooq, despite being a pro-Pakistan leader, did not use his separatist credentials to exploit the situation and convert it into an anti-India event; instead he ensured the maintenance of peace in the conflict-ridden state. May Allah grant him the highest place in Jannat.

UNEXECUTED WARRANT

As soon as Farooq Abdullah's government was unconstitutionally dismissed by Governor Jagmohan on 2 July 1984, as a result of the defections engineered by Prime Minister Indira Gandhi,[10,11,12] G.M. Shah, aka Gula Shah (Farooq's brother-in-law), was appointed as the chief minister. After the takeover, Shah's government announced its decision to issue a white paper against the Farooq government to highlight and expose his alleged misgovernance, corruption, secret alliance with anti-national parties and pro-Pakistan leaders and more. In a bid to collect the necessary material, Deputy CM Devi Das Thakur, one of the architects of the coup, took it upon himself to examine the files of various departments. I got a call that Thakur wanted to see me urgently. I complied and went to his office. Devi Das Thakur was very well known to me from his days at the Bar of the J&K High Court, as well as his tenure as a judge of the high court and a minister in Sheikh Abdullah's cabinet. I must admit he had always had great regard for me. As soon as I entered his office chamber, he received me courteously and called for tea.

---

[10]Widmalm, Sten, *Kashmir in Comparative Perspective—Democracy and Violent Separatism in India*, RoutledgeCurzon, London, 2002, 66–69.

[11]Nehru, Braj Kumar, *Nice Guys Finish Second*, Viking, New Delhi, 1997, 614.

[12]Chawla, Prabhu, 'Farooq Abdullah's Dramatic Dismissal as CM Throws J&K Into Acute Political Instability', *India Today*, 31 July 1984, https://www.indiatoday.in/magazine/cover-story/story/19840731-farooq-abdullahs-dramatic-dismissal-as-cm-throws-j-k-into-acute-political-instability-803189-1984-07-30. Accessed on 29 December 2023.

It may be recalled that to find an excuse to remove Farooq Abdullah, Indira Gandhi and her coterie in the state were hatching conspiracies to disturb peace and destabilize the region.[13,14,15] The state Congress party had activated their overt and covert activities against the Farooq government with the sole aim of removing him from power. They had also galvanized their propaganda machine in Delhi and within the state. Their attempts to disturb peace pushed the state police to fight a two-front war: one against the covert subversive activities of Pakistani agencies, and the other, as subsequent events would unfold, against the Indira Gandhi-backed local Congress activists who were determined to disturb the peace in the state, which suited the Pakistani establishment. Their propaganda machine was aided by corrupt national and local print media.

Having said this, I will share how one such gameplan was foiled by me to prevent disturbances in the Valley. Readers will surely understand to what extent the Congress high command, aided by intelligence agencies, stooped to disrupt peace and order to create an excuse to remove the Farooq government. To cause widespread disturbances in the state, central agencies played a very dangerous game. Without providing solid grounds, they

---

[13]Widmalm, Sten, *Kashmir in Comparative Perspective—Democracy and Violent Separatism in India*, RoutledgeCurzon, London, 2002, 66 69.

[14]Nehru, Braj Kumar, *Nice Guys Finish Second*, Viking, New Delhi, 1997, 614.

[15]Chawla, Prabhu, 'Farooq Abdullah's Dramatic Dismissal as CM Throws J&K Into Acute Political Instability', *India Today*, 31 July 1984, https://www.indiatoday.in/magazine/cover-story/story/19840731-farooq-abdullahs-dramatic-dismissal-as-cm-throws-j-k-into-acute-political-instability-803189-1984-07-30. Accessed on 29 December 2023.

wanted Syed Ali Shah Geelani to be arrested and detained.[16,17,18] Doing so would have set the state on fire. What Geelani was doing at that time was not the least prejudicial to the security of the state or the maintenance of public order. His routine speeches at the Friday namaz in different mosques of Sopore or other rural areas did not cause any adverse reaction from the public to justify his detention. The situation in the Valley was absolutely peaceful. Geelani's detention could disturb peace and cause large-scale violence throughout the Valley. To achieve their objective, I was asked to arrest Geelani and detain him under the Public Safety Act. I refused on the grounds that it would be counterproductive as the prevailing peaceful conditions in the Valley would be gravely disturbed. However, without further consultations with me and without my prior knowledge, an order of detention was issued by the government. Normally, such orders are issued by DCs on the request of a district SP. Although Geelani was permanently living in Sopore in those days, in an unusual act, the detention order was issued by the government to be executed by me as DIG, Kashmir Range. Under normal circumstances, such an order is given to the district SP or any of his subordinates. This was a plan to justify the dismissal of the Farooq government as it would cause large-scale disturbances and a breakdown of law and order. I was happy to see the order endorsed in my name because anyone else would have executed it

---

[16]Widmalm, Sten, *Kashmir in Comparative Perspective—Democracy and Violent Separatism in India*, RoutledgeCurzon, London, 2002, 66–69.

[17]Nehru, Braj Kumar, *Nice Guys Finish Second*, Viking, New Delhi, 1997, 614.

[18]Chawla, Prabhu, 'Farooq Abdullah's Dramatic Dismissal as CM Throws J&K into Acute Political Instability', *India Today*, 31 July 1984, https://www.indiatoday.in/magazine/cover-story/story/19840731-farooq-abdullahs-dramatic-dismissal-as-cm-throws-j-k-into-acute-political-instability-803189-1984-07-30. Accessed on 29 December 2023.

mechanically, without applying their mind regarding the possible adverse fallout.

Solely in the interest of peace and order, I decided not to act as a pawn of the Congress party. Notwithstanding my legal obligation, I deferred the execution on my own without my superiors' knowledge. I decided to act upon the order as and when absolutely necessary, according to my assessment of the situation. I didn't mention it even to the CM. Meanwhile, several months passed and nobody bothered to ask me why I had slept over the warrant. It was almost a forgotten issue because by that time, the Congress conspirators in Delhi and within the state had decided to play a bigger game. The Valley continued to be peaceful. Ultimately, Prime Minister Indira Gandhi succeeded and had the Farooq government dismissed by Governor Jagmohan on 2 July 1984.

Back to my meeting with Deputy CM Thakur Devi Das. After exchanging pleasantries, changed his tone abruptly and authoritatively asked me, 'Why did you not arrest Syed Ali Shah Geelani even though an order of detention was endorsed by the government to you for execution? Under whose orders did you defer his arrest?' The cat was out of the bag. My assessment was proved correct. This corroborated my belief that the detention order was motivated and the brainchild of the Congress leadership to destabilize the state and cause disturbances to justify the removal of Farooq's government. Otherwise, out of all the issues in the Farooq government, why did he decide to pick up this trivial matter of the non-execution of a warrant for a white paper? 'Sir, it was my decision to defer the execution of the order in the interest of the maintenance of peace and tranquillity in the Valley,' I told him. 'That is not true. You had no authority to flout government orders like this. Farooq Abdullah directed you not to execute the warrant, didn't he? He is hand in glove with pro-Pakistan leaders,' Thakur said threateningly, raising his voice a bit. Refusing to be browbeaten, I replied, 'Sir, he never asked me, and I never mentioned it to him. I repeat that neither Dr Farooq nor anyone in the police hierarchy told me not to arrest Geelani.' Thakur did not give up and even threatened me with dire consequences. I firmly told him, 'Sir, if you wish, you can record my statement. I will sign it, and you are free to take any action against me for flouting government orders. Under no circumstances will I deviate from the truth. It was my personal decision; that is all.' He suddenly calmed down, softened his attitude and said, 'I can understand your compulsions, but our government will be very happy if you cooperate.' I categorically told him that what I had said was true and that I could not deviate from the truth even if it cost me my career. I got up. We shook hands, and I left his room. The white paper he was supposed to prepare highlighting Dr Farooq Abdullah's alleged misdeeds never saw the light of day. Their only purpose was to corner him and defame him in the country as a pro-Pakistan collaborator.

I expected some serious action against me—at least my transfer—but nothing followed. The G.M. Shah government, at that crucial stage, may not have been able afford to replace me. I was never again questioned for this glaring dereliction of duty. Technically, yes, I had flouted a government order, but the order was issued behind my back without any request from me. As it was my responsibility to ensure peace and order in the Valley, in the interest of public peace, I decided not to execute the warrant.

It was my humble attempt to uphold the independence of the police, which the politicians of this country oppose tooth and nail to protect their political interests and continue to misuse the police to achieve their political ends. Since 2014, the country's police force and many other law enforcement agencies have been reduced to hired functionaries or private armies, with no respect for the badges of rank displayed on their uniform. They follow the law of lawlessness. Needless, to say Geelani was never made aware of this episode.

NOBODY LYNCHED AYUB PANDIT

This incident is a blot for Kashmiri separatist leaders, which they cannot wash off in this lifetime. An innocent life was tortured and lynched due to the madness infused in the youth on Shab-e-Qadr, the 27th night of the holy month of Ramzan (corresponding to 21 June 2017, in Saudi Arabia and 22/23 June 2017, in India), which is the most sacred night for Muslims worldwide. On this night, the holy Quran was revealed to Prophet Muhammad (SAW). Believers seek forgiveness for their sins from the Almighty without sleeping a wink. This is a night for repentance, submission, contrition, penitence, remorsefulness, praying and pleading guilty before the Lord in all humility.

On that sacred night of June 2017, I was at Madina, Saudi Arabia, praying at Masjid-e-Nabi (Prophet's Mosque) amidst Aietiqaaf (retreat to pray in a mosque for a particular number of days and nights). My companions from Kashmir on this holy journey told me that according to the news circulated on social media, an officer of the J&K Police had been lynched by an unruly mob at Jamia Masjid, Srinagar, on the night of Shab-e-Qadr. As my companions and I were in a different state of mind at that moment, we did not go into the details, but were very sad. Normally, nobody can even think of harming any fellow human being or living creature on such an auspicious and precious night. I believe that the Almighty will not forgive the culprits responsible for this dastardly and inhuman crime.

Back in Srinagar, I found out that my son Shafqat, IGP Armed Police at Jammu, had posted a blog on Facebook, which gives an idea about how anguished the police officers were.

WHAT NEXT?

S.A. Watali

During the intervening night of 22–23 June 2017, we lost our beloved Mohammad Ayub deputy SP while performing his duties in Srinagar. Our hero was killed brutally by a mob of insane people who transformed into a group of frenzied barbarians. This brave officer, even in his death, maintained the true values of our force and left the flag of J&K Police untainted. He exhibited total restraint. He could have easily killed a few of those criminals with his service revolver while trying to save himself knowing full well that he had no chance of survival. We all are still in shock as are all the peace-loving citizens of the state and country. However, none of us can even fathom the sense of loss that his family members must be feeling. All of us are numb. All of us are angry and rightly so, and many of us have openly expressed our feelings and sense of shock over this tragic and shocking loss. Now, the question arises: what next? What do we want individually and collectively? Do we want justice or revenge? The answer is that we want justice. Let us remember that we are being tested in this time of grave crisis and grief. The real test of our values comes at such times of grave loss and provocation. However, the sacrifice of my brother Mohammad Ayub should not go waste. His killers must face the gallows for this dastardly and merciless killing.

> We need to maintain the dignity and values we dearly cherish. We should not allow our anger and pain to overpower us. Let us pause a bit and think and give a dignified response to this undignified, disgraceful and inhuman act. Let us exhibit our true professional calibre and investigate this case in a way that the killers meet their fate as per the law of the land. We owe it to our brave comrade. A foolproof case, being the rarest of the rare, investigated in a truly professional manner must end in a death sentence. Let us not allow the death of Mohammad Ayub to make us bitter, revengeful or negative. We are not at war with anyone. We are protectors, not killers. Our job is to uphold the law, and this is our chance to show how the law of the land is upheld and how the supremacy of the law is ensured. That is the only way to get justice; that's the only way to restore the dignity of the Khaki. We must not act to avenge, but we must act to ensure justice. We must remain what we are, a people's police force with a heart of gold and the resolve of steel. Let us be careful and ensure that we do not become bloodthirsty monsters. This is the time to tightly hold on to our values, ethos and great virtues that we have imbibed by toiling and working hard to restore peace in our troubled land. The killers have stooped too low, but we must not go down to their level. This is the time to rise, not fall.

Such was the anguish expressed and conveyed by a senior police officer, who, at the same time, advised his colleagues not to be revengeful but investigate the case thoroughly and impartially so that the real culprits were brought to justice and punished.

What transpired on that auspicious night at Jamia Masjid, Srinagar, was an act of sheer savagery. I don't believe that the people who had come to pray and ask for forgiveness for their sins on this holy night could have committed such a dastardly act and unforgivable sin of lynching Deputy SP Mohammad Ayub Pandit. Ayub was on security duty in charge of access control at the main gate of Jamia Masjid to protect senior Hurriyat leader Mirwaiz Omar Farooq, who was scheduled to address the gathering on the importance of the holy night. I was told that the unruly mob caught hold of him inside the mosque gate, attacked him, battered him ruthlessly and dragged him out of the mosque like a log of wood. They snatched away his service revolver and looted an amount of ₹40,000 from his person, which he had reportedly drawn from the bank to spend during Eid celebrations with his family. In my whole life, I have never come across such a ghastly and inhuman crime committed by a mob of savages masquerading as humans.

In my capacity as an ex-member of the state police force, I was naturally keen to know exactly what had happened and why the victim could not be saved by the powerful J&K Police and other security forces who had all the required resources at their disposal. Why did no officer from the more than one lakh strong state police force care to rescue him? Why had it happened? I was trying to find the answers to too many questions as a former cop. I was told that the area and the concerned SHO had been attached, as a punishment after this gruesome incident, probably as a cover up.

On 21 September 2017, by sheer chance, I ran into an old friend, well-wisher and senior advocate of the J&K High Court, Mohammad Sultan Pandit, when I happened to be at the district court in Srinagar for a personal matter. As soon as he saw me, he hugged me affectionately. Both of us went into the nearby prosecution office and chatted about our mutual experiences during my active service. While talking to him, I was shocked to learn that the martyred Ayub Pandit was his younger brother.

Sultan told me that Ayub had left behind his widow, a son and a daughter. Now, the son was looking after the ancestral vocation of seed farming, which had considerably shrunk due to the partition of ancestral land. His daughter was pursuing her MBBS in Bangalore. I was surprised when he told me that Ayub had been recruited as an SI in the police department during my tenure as a member of the recruitment board. I had not a clue about his recruitment, but I felt additionally hurt about how one of my selectees had met a tragic and gruesome end at the hands of the mob within the precincts of the greatest mosque in the city. While talking to Sultan, I decided to make his tragic story a part of this book so that coming generations, particularly in the police, shall know about Ayub's sacrifice as a police officer and about the shameful conduct and cowardice displayed by his fellow officers and colleagues.

Sultan informed me that as soon as Ayub came to his house late on the fateful night, he got a message on his walkie-talkie to proceed to Jamia Masjid, where he was supposed to perform access control duty at the main gate as a security measure for the protection of Mirwaiz Umar Farooq, a senior Hurriyat leader. Two constables were detailed with Ayub to assist him. Police sources told me that he was routinely put on this duty on Fridays whenever Mirwaiz was scheduled to deliver his sermon. Jamia Masjid is hardly 2 km away from Ayub's residence. Before leaving his house, he had told his wife that he would return after midnight, Sultan informed me. He also told me that after assuming his duty, he had allowed his two assistants to leave early when he felt that everything was normal. It was a kind gesture on Ayub's part to allow his subordinates to spend the rest of this holy night in prayers with their family.

An eyewitness revealed to me that after some time, a group of youths, who may not have been there for the prayers, reportedly surrounded him and asked him to show his identity card. Ayub retorted, 'Who are you to ask me to show my identity card?' Undeterred, he refused to be pressurized and resisted their uncalled-for demand. Suddenly, one of the goons from among the group struck him on the back of his neck with his fist. Ayub fell on the mosque floor and his weapon, which had been tucked in his pants, was exposed. The attackers attempted to snatch the weapon, but Ayub held it firmly and refused to part with it. The scuffle resulted in an accidental fire from the revolver, which caused the testicles of one of the attackers to be blown off and injured another attacker. The gunshots obviously attracted more people. The group of monsters around him swelled into a large crowd who were successful in snatching away his revolver.

Ayub was attacked by scores of them with no holds barred. They were battering and kicking his limbs and vital organs. Dragging him out of the mosque like a log, they beat him with whatever they could get hold of within the compound. The murderous mob took turns to climb over the mosque's boundary wall to jump on his body, one by one breaking, crushing and dislocating his bones. They literally converted his body into pulp. Their bestiality knew no bounds as they continued to violently assault his dead body. Finally, in the wee hours of the morning, they threw his body on the main road near a Bata Shoes showroom at Nowhatta Chowk.

Mirwaiz is said to have arrived at the mosque at about midnight. I am sure he must have been informed about the ghastly incident, but he chose not to speak about it during his sermon. His silence could be interpreted as approving what had happened. How could he ignore such a dastardly crime against humanity, that too in a mosque? Mirwaiz could have expressed a few words of sympathy for the man who was killed in the line of duty, protecting him.

My inquiries from reliable sources revealed that the entire night, the police force deployed for duty, comprising several companies, was invisible, presumably concealed within the confines of the two police stations of Khanyar and Nowhatta. I was told that they were strictly ordered by the senior officer in charge not to venture out for fear of inviting stone-pelting with their presence. What strange logic! Policing in absentia? Some well-meaning citizens are said to have informed the PCR as soon as Ayub was attacked as the PCR was reportedly flooded with messages from the public. However no action was taken as no policeman came to the spot even in civvies to verify the information, let alone come to Ayub's rescue. The PCR must have routinely disseminated the information received from the public to the concerned officers responsible for maintaining law and order during that night but nobody rose to the occasion to save their colleague's precious life. Nothing but unprecedented cowardice was displayed by the top- and middle-level leadership of the J&K Police, who left their colleague at the mercy of bloodthirsty vultures.

In the morning, the PCR is said to have been informed about a death, not of Deputy SP Ayub but of some unknown Bihari labourer. Shakespeare's description of Caesar's murder from *Julius Caesar* comes to mind: the most unkindest cut of all. Ayub seemed to have been neglected, ignored and forgotten not only by his immediate boss, who had deputed him for duty, and the jurisdictional officers but also by the entire chain of command up to the top. My research on the matter revealed that all the gazetted officers of the police, who were on duty on that fateful night, were concealing themselves at the Khanyar Police Station about half a kilometre away, where they were just whiling away their time gossiping, oblivious to what was happening to their colleague. It was also revealed by unconfirmed sources that on receiving information from the PCR, the Nowhatta SHO wanted to go to the spot but was refused permission to intervene in the situation even though he had sufficient manpower at his disposal to save Ayub. They very well knew that Ayub was being lynched by the mob. An assault by a few companies could have been launched from various directions to rescue our martyr, Ayub Pandit.

It is standard procedure for the police to make special arrangements on festivals even in times of peace. Night patrolling is also conducted on such occasions. Plain-clothes officers are deployed by the CID and District Special Branch around and inside important mosques and shrines. Where were all these officers? Nobody has an answer. I am sure that CID sleuths must have informed their hierarchy about the attack on Ayub Pandit. No information was provided. Everything was shrouded in mystery. The silence, a criminal silence, was deafening. Even the uniformed police guard, permanently mounted at Jamia Masjid, did not intervene to save the life of their officer; it is unknown whether they informed anyone. Knowledgeable sources disclosed that there was no shortage of manpower either around Jamia Masjid or in the entire city, particularly in downtown Srinagar as per the standard operating procedure (SOP) The police had faced stone pelting in this area on Shab-e-Qadr since 2011. Since then, troops are always deployed as per the SOP.

On the fateful night of 22–23 June 2017, the police, instead of facing the mob to save their colleague, ignored their SOP and chose to remain invisible for fear of stone pelters. They did not even verify the reports received from the PCR. They simply hid within the four walls of the police stations. This was nothing but cowardice of the highest order, which was unheard of!

Though the PCR was informed about the death of a Bihari labourer around 5 a.m., Faheem, the deputy SP in charge of Mirwaiz's security detail, reportedly visited the PCR and identified the dead body of Mohammad Ayub Pandit on his own. He then informed the officers that it was the body found was of Ayub Pandit and not that of a Bihari labourer. Why and under what circumstances Faheem had gone to the PCR so early in the morning is a matter of suspicion. Was he silenced by powers within the police force or by some other influential lobby? Faheem's conduct needs to be probed. He seems to be guilty of negligence and cowardice in performing his duty. Being on duty with Mirwaiz, he was certainly an eyewitness to the gory episode but remained a silent spectator.

As soon as the PCR transferred Faheem's report to the concerned authorities, everyone from top to bottom turned to self-preservation. Were they trying to look for an excuse to convert the story of a Bihari labourer's death to that of one of their own officers being the victim? Ayub Pandit was a victim of a new police doctrine, the doctrine of policing in absentia.

To cover up this criminal inaction, an FIR was registered based on a reliable report (unnamed eyewitness) that strangely identified the alleged culprits by name, parentage and residential address. How could this be a reliable source report? Who was the so-called reliable secret source? Was it a person who could give detailed particulars about the accused persons to the SHO the same night that he and his staff had taken cover in a well-guarded police station? The reliable source could be a police officer who had witnessed the occurrence but not acted. No civilian source could possibly know all the accused, their parentage and their residential addresses across the city. Why was the case not registered at the earliest on the basis of the repeated messages received from the PCR, following standard procedure that carries more weight under the law?

The fate of the case was a foregone conclusion. Ayub's

revolver is said to have been recovered from another unknown reliable person, who was not listed as an accused. The case was reportedly dealt with without proper investigation by the police and presented before the court hastily. This was probably done to shield the negligent officers from facing an inquiry and punishment with the excuse that the case was sub judice. They perhaps didn't know that notwithstanding the case being sub judice, a departmental inquiry is not barred from pinpointing the culpability and criminal negligence of the concerned officers.

Didn't poor Ayub Pundit's dastardly death deserve a judicial inquiry or even an open departmental inquiry to pinpoint the responsibility of various officers on duty and to take action against the guilty? Because the entire police hierarchy from top to bottom was involved, the police leadership indulged in self-deception to believe that nobody lynched Ayub Pandit. This is the fate of all cases wherein our unsung heroes, that is, police officials or their kith and kin, were killed in cold blood by militants and unknown gunmen. None of the culprits have been punished in over three decades. Even the broad daylight killing of my younger brother, Dr Gulshan Watali, in June 1990 was not investigated, although the culprits had been identified and prima facie evidence to arrest and prosecute them had been gathered. Notwithstanding sufficient evidence on record, I am pained to state that an IGP closed the case as untraced, apparently due to monetary considerations.

Chapter 4

Freedom Movement in PoK

Azad Kashmir came into existence with a declaration issued by its provisional government on 24 October 1947. Its 'capital', Pulandari, is a small town south of Poonch. The declaration envisaged the territory as an independent entity. It expressed 'sentiments of the utmost friendliness and goodwill towards neighbouring Dominions of India and Pakistan and hopes that both the Dominions will sympathize with the people of Jammu and Kashmir in their efforts to exercise their birthright of political freedom.'[19] The Declaration of Azad Kashmir is word by word a declaration of an independent Jammu and Kashmir.

Had Pakistani rulers been really serious about the state's azadi, they would have honoured the declaration and granted freedom to PoK, which had an area of 13,297 square km and a population of 40,45,366 as per the 2017 national census.[20] Had they been sincere, they could have declared the territory under their control as an independent country and sought recognition from a few friendly sovereign countries. Meanwhile, Pakistan would look after the defence of the newly created country through a mutual agreement.

However, this did not happen. Initially, there was no

---

[19]Khan, Sardar M. Ibrahim, *The Kashmir Saga*, Ripon Print Press, Lahore, 1965, 41–119.

[20]Azad Government of the State of Jammu & Kashmir, https://ajk.gov.pk/. Accessed on 4 September 2023.

constitution and mere Rules of Business governed the affairs of PoK. However, in October 1952, the Rules of Business were amended to say, 'The President shall hold office during the pleasure of the General Council of the All Jammu and Kashmir Muslim Conference, duly recognized as such by the Government of Pakistan and the Ministry of Kashmir Affairs.' In this manner, the declaration of an independent state was diluted and the Azad Kashmir government was downgraded to a powerless body under the all-powerful Ministry of Kashmir Affairs. The Azad Kashmir Constitution debars all those who do not subscribe to the state's accession to Pakistan from contesting elections to the assembly. The people residing in PoK do not enjoy any rights guaranteed under the Constitution of Pakistan to the people of other provinces. The recent move by the Government of Pakistan to fully annex Gilgit–Baltistan as the fifth province further highlights the dichotomy of Pakistan's Kashmir policy.

The fact is that neither India nor Pakistan ever favoured an independent country of J&K at their respective borders. Azad Kashmir remains an administrative unit under Pakistan with its own president, chief minister, separate constitution and an assembly. A body called Azad Kashmir Council, with the prime minister of Pakistan as its head, wields overriding powers. This council has the power to nullify any law or resolution passed by the duly elected assembly of PoK.

Eventually, a section of Kashmiris in Pakistan and PoK were confronted with a situation where they thought that complete independence of the state was the most suitable and acceptable formula for the people living in the two separate parts of the state. The trigger was the dismissal and arrest of their prime minister, Sheikh Mohammad Abdullah, by the GoI on 9 August 1953. Influenced by the subsequent developments in the state,

Ghulam Mohammad Lone, a Kashmiri businessman in Karachi, and K.H. Khurshid, a Muslim Conference leader of the state and a practising barrister who had earlier been opposed to Sheikh Mohammad Abdullah, organized protest demonstrations in Karachi and other parts of Pakistan against his arrest. Khurshid had also served as the private secretary to Quaid-e-Azam Muhammad Ali Jinnah before Partition. Later, he was elected as the president of PoK and subsequently arrested by Pakistani authorities after his dismissal. Reportedly, Lone had mobilized all Kashmiris living in Sindh. In due course, he was joined by two other prominent and erstwhile residents of Jammu, namely, Mir Abdul Qayoom and his brother Mir Abdul Mannan.

In 1961, during Khurshid's rule, Lone was elected as a member of the Azad Kashmir State Council. In his election manifesto, Lone declared that Kashmir was not merely a border dispute between India and Pakistan but was about the right of self-determination of its people, even though under the election law, anyone who did not subscribe to the accession of the state to Pakistan could not contest elections.

On 12 May 1963, in a meeting of Kashmiri intellectuals and political workers held at Hotel Dawn, Rawalpindi, a resolution demanding an independent state of Jammu and Kashmir was unanimously adopted. The participants also formed the Kashmir Independence Committee (KIC), with G.M. Lone as the convener. The members included Mir Abdul Qayoom of Jammu, Advocate Abdul Khaliq Ansari from Mirpur, Qazi Khurshid Alam, Abdul Majid Malik, Amanullah Khan, Mir Abdul Aziz from the Kashmir Valley, Mir Abdul Rashid, Majeed Amjad, Ghulam Nabi Gilkar (senior leader of the J&K Muslim Conference), Sheikh Mohammad Saleem, Advocate M.A. Farooq, Syed Sayeed Shah Nazki of the Kashmir Valley, Dr Ghulam Ahmad Jarrah and Ghulam

Mohammad Malik.[21] This marked an ideological paradigm shift as all these individuals had been staunch supporters of the state's accession to Pakistan before migrating from India and settling in PoK/Pakistan. With the formation of the KIC, the demand for azadi was formalized, much to the annoyance of Pakistani and PoK authorities.

The idea of an independent Kashmir was not new. In fact, the Naya Kashmir resolution of 1944 was nothing short of a constitution for a free state of Jammu and Kashmir under the Maharaja. Even the Muslim Conference, despite being a pro-Pakistan party, had publicly proposed an independent Kashmir in 1947. The NC and Muslim Conference wanted Maharaja Hari Sigh to be a constitutional head. Giving details of his meeting with Chaudhry Abbas, an imprisoned leader of the Muslim Conference, Sheikh Mohammad Abdullah, writes[22]:

> We concluded that a plebiscite, if at all held, would lead to further bloodshed. Of course, the situation might improve if India and Pakistan guaranteed the state's independence [...] So I told him, once in Pakistan, he should persuade Jinnah to agree to the proposal we had thought out. Later, it was discovered that he had put the proposal before Jinnah, but the latter had rejected it [...] There was, however, a large group of workers, headed by Choudhry Hamidullah Khan, the acting president of the All Jammu and Kashmir Muslim Conference, in favour of the state remaining independent of both India and Pakistan.

Meanwhile, a young Kashmiri man and student of Government

---

[21]Saraf, Muhammad Yusuf, *Kashmiris Fight for Freedom, Vol. 2 (1947–1978)*, Ferozsons, Lahore, 1979, 1378.

[22]Abdullah, Sheikh Mohammad, *The Blazing Chinar: An Autobiography*, Gulshan Books, Srinagar, 2013, 313.

Degree College, Baramulla, Kashmir, Maqbool Ahmed Bhat, of Trehgam village in present-day Kupwara district of the Kashmir Valley, emerged on the scene in 1958. As a student, Maqbool was largely influenced by the political ideology of Sheikh Mohammad Abdullah. Sheikh's release from prison in December 1957 and his subsequent rearrest triggered a chain of agitation and political activities in the state. Maqbool became actively involved in these activities. Fearing arrest, he went underground till his BA results were announced. With his results declared, he managed to get his provisional BA certificate from the college and crossed over to PoK in August 1958, accompanied by his uncle Abdul Aziz Butt. After exploring various places in Pakistan in search of a livelihood, he ultimately settled in Peshawar. There, he continued his studies and simultaneously adopted journalism as his profession. He worked as a news editor for the Peshawar-based *Anjaam* and the daily *Bang-e-Haram*. Later, he was also the editor of the weekly, *Khyber Mail*. Meanwhile, he completed his MA in Urdu Literature from Peshawar University. A born revolutionary with a restless urge for azadi, he came into contact with some members of the KIC. In early 1965, Advocate Abdul Khaliq Ansari, Amanullah Khan, Mannan, G.M. Lone, G.M. Mir (another Kashmiri migrant hailing from Duroo Shahabad in the Kashmir Valley) and Maqbool Bhat held a brainstorming session in Mirpur for several days to form a political party. They approached some Pakistan- and PoK-based senior Kashmiri leaders for advice; however, the leaders distanced themselves from the idea of forming a party to secure complete independence and not for accession to Pakistan.[23]

---

[23]Saraf, Muhammad Yusuf, *Kashmiris Fight for Freedom, Vol. 2 (1947–1978)*, Ferozsons, Lahore, 1979, 1378.

The J&K Plebiscite Front, which demanded a plebiscite to ascertain the will of the people under the supervision of the UNSC, had already been launched by Mirza Afzal Beg in 1955 under the patronage of the incarcerated Sheikh Mohammad Abdullah. The PF rose as a popular organization with widespread support in the Valley and parts of Jammu. The party was mainly a conglomerate of cadres of erstwhile NC members, some youth groups and some erstwhile pro-Pakistan leaders who had earlier been opposed to Sheikh Abdullah. With time, the organization caught the imagination of all pro-azadi masses of PoK. The Azadi Movement in PoK got a shot in the arm when they held a huge public meeting of Kashmiris in Sialkot, Pakistan, in the vicinity of the Sucheetgarh border near Jammu on 3 and 4 April 1965. They announced the formation of the J&K Plebiscite Front, PoK, with Abdul Khaliq Ansari as president and the aim to secure an independent state of Jammu and Kashmir.

After some time, the PF leadership of PoK lost faith in the peaceful struggle of the parent body in the Valley. Therefore, Maqbool Ahmed Bhat and Major Amanullah Khan formed the National Liberation Front (NLF) as an underground armed wing of the PF. Its objective was to launch an armed struggle to liberate the state. Maqbool strongly believed that the state could not be liberated unless Kashmiris picked up arms. The NLF, however, became unpopular with the Pakistan establishment as well as the PoK administration. They did not relish the formation of any organization other than the one advocating for the accession of the state to Pakistan. Therefore, to defame the organization, Pakistani agencies always branded Maqbool and his colleagues as Indian agents.

After the fiasco of Operation Gibraltar in 1965, an NLF group led by Maqbool Ahmed Bhat and consisting of Major Amanullah Khan, Subedar Kalay Khan, Aurangzeb, a young man from

Gilgit–Baltistan, and Mir Ahmed, a porter, crossed the CFL into the Valley on 21 June 1966 through Lashdat, situated between Safawali and Manigah in the northern hills of the Valley. Major Amanullah Khan, who originally belonged to a feudal family of Haihama, Kupwara, had served as a major in the British Indian Army during the Second World War. He was reportedly taken prisoner by the Japanese. Like other Indian POWs, he had joined Subhas Chandra Bose's Indian National Army to liberate India from the British by helping the Japanese in the war.

As a schoolboy, I had the occasion to see Major Amanullah in 1945–46 in Handwara. His brother, Inayatullah Khan, had been my batchmate in high school. Major Amanullah had been released following his acquittal in the Red Fort trial, wherein Indian National Army officers were tried by a special tribunal. Jawaharlal Nehru, Bhulabhai Desai and other eminent lawyers of the Congress party had represented them at the trail. After his release and return to his home, Major Amanullah joined the timber business in Kupwara. Following the Pakistani tribal attack, Major Amanullah Khan had reportedly joined the raiders in October 1947 and fought against the Indian Army. After their defeat, he crossed over to PoK along with his father Saifullah Khan, his brothers, including my friend Inayatullah, and other male members of his extended family. Their womenfolk and children, who were left behind, were later sent to Pakistan in an officially sponsored convoy via Suchetgarh, Jammu, as a humanitarian gesture with the help and good offices of my father, Haji Ghulam Nabi Watali, who was then a prominent leader of the NC at Handwara.

After infiltrating into the Valley in June 1966, Major Amanullah established his base at Haihama, Kupwara, and did not move to the hinterland. However, Maqbool reportedly visited almost all the important towns and many villages of the

Valley, where he met his old friends and batchmates from school and college, particularly in the erstwhile undivided districts of Baramulla and Srinagar. Many of them joined him in his covert mission as they were convinced by his ideology of armed struggle for the liberation of the state. Within a short period of about three months, he is believed to have established a tight-knit underground cell of the NLF in the Valley; the police, army, other security forces and intelligence agencies remained blissfully ignorant.

Maqbool Bhat succeeded in sowing the seeds of an armed struggle for azadi in the Valley. His ideology gave a shot in the arm to the post-1965 war underground armed resistance movement already initiated by Kashmiri youth. Maqbool reportedly circulated two documents among his supporters clandestinely. One was a declaration purported to be issued on behalf of the people of undivided Jammu and Kashmir, including Ladakh and Gigot, announcing them as free people and declaring war against all those who deprived the people of freedom. He also introduced the NLF to lead and supervise future 'collective actions' to achieve freedom. The second, which was issued simultaneously, was a statement reiterating his slogan of armed struggle for liberation. His statement gave a clear idea about his secular outlook. Maqbool did not espouse any Islamist or jihadi ideology. While declaring war against the Indian state, Maqbool said, 'The people of this state, irrespective of caste, creed, colour and religion, are our fighters, and every Kashmiri is coming to fight for the liberation of this motherland.' Needless to say, he did not get any support from the Pakistani establishment.

Mohammad Azam Inqilabi's (Mohammad Altaf Khan) experience during his first meeting with Maqbool in Muzaffarabad, PoK, throws sufficient light on Maqbool's secular ideology. Inqilabi asked Bhat, 'Why have you named the armed wing of the PF National Liberation Front? Why not Muslim Liberation Front?' Bhat replied, 'We want our non-Muslim brethren to join our resistance movement also.' Regarding another incident, Inqilabi said, 'Amanullah Khan asked me to become a member of the NLF by signing an oath of allegiance with my blood. I agreed and started writing my name, suffixed with "Bismillahi Rahman e Raheem". Aman sahib objected, and I had to sign a fresh form.'[24] This incident underscores the secular character of Maqbool and Amanullah Khan's ideology.

Maqbool's underground group surfaced and came to the notice of the authorities as well as the media only when state CID official Amar Chand was knifed to death at Nadihal, his ancestral village near Baramulla. At midnight, Amar Chand was allegedly called out of his house by one Mohammad Dar, a double agent. Immediately thereafter, the state police and paramilitary forces launched a manhunt and tracked the group to somewhere in the Rafiabad area of Baramulla in west Kashmir. After a brief encounter, Maqbool, Kalay Khan and other members of their group were reportedly arrested on 16 September 1966. However, Aurangzeb, one of their comrades-in-arms from Gilgit–Baltistan, was allegedly killed in the encounter. On receiving this news, Major Amanullah, who had stayed put in his home village of Haihama, Kupwara, is understood to have recrossed the CFL into PoK. Subsequently, Major Amanullah reportedly died in Peshawar where he had settled.

Maqbool Bhat and Kalay Khan were tried in a special court in Srinagar and were convicted. Maqbool was awarded the death sentence, whereas Kalay Khan was sentenced to life imprisonment. However, while on death row in Srinagar Central

---

[24]Inqilabi, Mohammad Azam, *Payam-e-Hurriyat*, Glob Group Printers, Srinagar, 2006, 32.

Jail, Maqbool and two of his cell mates, Mir Ahmed and Ayub, allegedly dug a hole in the northern wall of the jail and escaped. The government deployed all resources and even announced a cash reward for any information leading to their arrest, but they could not be traced. It was later learnt that they were assisted by the common people who helped them cross over to PoK through the treacherous and difficult north-western route of Tutmari Gali in the Kazinag mountain range during the harsh winter. He and his companions were reportedly taken into custody by the Pakistani Army as soon as they crossed the LoC. Maqbool and his comrades were reportedly detained at Muzaffarabad Fort, where they were allegedly subjected to unprecedented physical, mental and psychological torture, insult and humiliation. The Pakistani interrogators experimented with unique torture techniques on their persons. They accused Maqbool and his associates of being Indian agents. They never believed his story of having escaped from the heavily guarded Srinagar jail. However, Maqbool Bhat was cleared of all charges and released after three months.

Maqbool Bhat contested elections in PoK in 1970, only to be defeated in suspected rigged polls. According to a former leader of the Jammu Kashmir Liberation Front (JKLF) who served as Bhat's polling agent in Rawalpindi in the 1970s, non-Kashmiris were allowed to vote (for a seat exclusively meant for Kashmiri migrants) to ensure that Maqbool Bhat did not win.[25] Maqbool's goal of an independent state of Jammu and Kashmir was always opposed by the Pakistani establishment.[26]

On 30 January 1971, Indian Airlines' Fokker Friendship plane travelling from Srinagar to Delhi was hijacked by two

---

[25]Saraf, Muhammad Yusuf, *Kashmiris Fight for Freedom, Vol. 2 (1947–1978)*, Ferozsons, Lahore, 1979, 1378.

[26]Asad, Mohammad Saeed, *Deewanon Pe Kya Guzri*, National Institute of Kashmir Studies, Mirpur, 2012, 101, 142–150.

Kashmiris, Hashim Qureshi and his cousin Ashraf. The plane was set on fire at Lahore airport after the crew and passengers were rescued by Pakistani authorities and sent to Delhi. Maqbool joined the hijackers in Lahore, who were taken in a procession by the huge crowds as genuine freedom fighters of Kashmir. Zulfiqar Ali Bhutto also met the hijackers at Lahore airport, where they again received a hero's welcome as Kashmiri freedom fighters. However, this honour was short-lived.

A preliminary inquiry carried out in Srinagar the same day established that Hashim Qureshi was a BSF sub-inspector. A copy of his appointment order to the BSF was recovered by the police from his home. This fact was leaked from someone at a senior level in the state, which was then published in the national press. Subsequently, India closed airspace to Pakistani planes in response to the hijacking and burning of the Indian plane, which ultimately culminated in the 1971 war and the creation of Bangladesh. Thereafter, Pakistani authorities suspected that the hijackers were sponsored by Maqbool Bhat and his NLF associates in Pakistan who were Indian agents. This assessment was based on a report prepared by a committee of two ISI officers and a dismissed civil servant. Accordingly, Maqbool Ahmed Bhat, Abdul Khaliq Ansari, G.M. Lone, Mir Abdul Qayoom, Mir Abdul Mannan, Hashim Qureshi, Ashraf Qureshi and Peerzada Ghulam Mustafa Alvi were arrested and brutally tortured in the dark and dingy cells of Dulai Camp, Muzaffarabad, Shahi Qila, Lahore, and Karachi's Special Staff lock-ups by police and security officials. Innovative, inhuman, dirty and brutal methods of torture were used on the arrested suspects just to extract a confession that they were Indian agents and had hijacked the Ganga[27] according

---

[27]Ganga is the Indian Airlines domestic Fokker F27 that was hijacked by Hashim Qureshi and his cousin, Ashraf.

to the instructions of Indian authorities. A few of them even succumbed to the torture and falsely confessed as ordered.[28]

Later, they were tried before a special tribunal comprising Justice Yaqub Ali Khan of the Pakistan Supreme Court and Justice Abdul Kader, a senior judge of the Sindh Balochistan High Court. The tribunal held the PF and NLF as 'patriotic' organizations. Hashim Qureshi was held to be an agent of Indian intelligence agencies and was convicted. The rest of the accused, including Maqbool Bhat, were declared freedom fighters and acquitted.[29]

Notably, on 10 September 1976, another Indian Airlines Boeing 737 travelling from Delhi to Jaipur was hijacked by another group of Kashmiris headed by Abdul Hameed Dewani of Bandipore; this flight also landed at Lahore airport. All the six hijackers on board, Abdul Hameed Dewani, Ghulam Nabi Yattoo of Qazigund, Ghulam Rasool Shaheen, Mohammad Ahsan, Mohammad Rafeiq and Abdul Rashid—all from Shopian—were Kashmiris. Dewani, an emotionally committed Azadi activist in PoK, was later detained by Pakistani authorities and imprisoned at Chilas Jail in Gilgit–Baltistan. He reportedly died unsung and unwept in PoK.[30]

After Maqbool was released from Muzaffarabad Fort in May 1973, his restless passion for freedom motivated him to cross over into the Valley again along with his two teen associates, Reyaz Dar and Hamid Bhat. He was aware of the hangman's noose waiting for him as he had cheated the gallows by escaping from Srinagar Jail. However, on reaching Langate, a town near

---

[28]Asad, Mohammad Saeed, *Deewanon Pe Kya Guzri*, National Institute of Kashmir Studies, Mirpur, 2012, 101, 142–150.

[29]Watali, Ali Mohammad, *Kashmir Intifada: A Memoir*, Gulshan Books, Srinagar, 2016, 137, 138, 315–19.

[30]Saraf, Muhammad Yusuf, *Kashmiris Fight for Freedom, Vol. 2 (1947–1978)*, Ferozsons, Lahore, 1979, 1382.

Handwara, he got entangled with a bank manager and allegedly shot him dead. Maqbool reportedly fled from the spot. Without knowing his identity, the agitated people of the locality followed him and his companions. They were apprehended with the help of the local police. Later, the GoI ordered his transfer to Tihar Jail, New Delhi, where he was confined in a death row cell, though the Langate case against him was sub judice in a Srinagar court.

Meanwhile, on 6 February 1984, Ravinder Mhatre, an Indian diplomat, was kidnapped in London. An unknown underground organization, the Kashmir Liberation Army, took responsibility for the kidnapping and demanded the release of Maqbool Bhat, his companions and some other prisoners. Indira Gandhi rejected the demand, and Mhatre was killed in Birmingham. The situation was aggravated, and the GoI hanged Maqbool on 11 February 1984. He was buried inside the Tihar Jail.[31] His hanging did not attract any major reaction in the Valley, except some low-key demonstrations in Sopore and Trehgam, his home town. JI Kashmir also did not give any importance to his hanging. Srinagar was absolutely peaceful. There was no notable reaction in Pakistan either. Moreover, the Pakistani government never tried to get him released through diplomatic channels before his execution when he was lodged in Tihar Jail for several years. Had they been interested in doing so, they could have easily swapped him with any Indian prisoner lodged in any Pakistani jail.

Against all odds, the Kashmir National Party was formed by pro-azadi groups in PoK long ago to spearhead the freedom movement. The Kashmir National Party, which was headed

---

[31] Saraf, Muhammad Yusuf, *Kashmiris Fight for Freedom, Vol. 2 (1947–1978)*, Ferozsons, Lahore, 1979, 1382.

by Afzal Sulehria, was not even allowed to carry out peaceful activities. Sulehria told *Al Jazeera* that he had been jailed three times and faced court cases for the last sixteen years for having advocated for an independent Kashmir. He and other political activists also told *Al Jazeera* that they had been charged with treason or sedition by Pakistani authorities. 'We are not citizens of Pakistan as per the Pakistan constitution, the United Nations resolutions and our own laws,' said Sulehria.[32] 'Our slogans were that Kashmir should have the right to self-determination, and India and Pakistani forces should leave Kashmir,' Toqeer Gilani, the Pakistani chief of the JKLF, told *Al Jazeera*. He continued, 'Pakistan's suppression of pro-freedom narratives is akin to India's position.'[33]

Human rights violations in Azad Kashmir have been a cause of concern, encompassing forced disappearances, alleged torture, political suppression and electoral manipulation. The Human Rights Commission of Pakistan reports that the ISI conducts widespread surveillance of the media and pro-freedom organizations. Instances of arbitrary arrests and torture resulting in fatalities have also been documented. In 2006, Brad Adams, the Asia director of *Human Rights Watch*, said, 'Although azad means free, the residents of Azad Kashmir are anything but free.'[34] Although suppressed, a vibrant freedom movement demanding azadi from India and Pakistan in accordance with their aspirations is active in Azad Kashmir. In my perspective,

---

[32]Hashim, Asad, 'In Pakistan-administered Kashmir, a Shrinking Pro-freedom Space', *Al Jazeera*, 4 March 2019, https://www.aljazeera.com/news/2019/3/4/in-pakistan-administered-kashmir-a-shrinking-pro-freedom-space. Accessed on 13 February 2024.

[33]Ibid.

[34]'Pakistan: "Free Kashmir" Far From Free', *Human Rights Watch*, 21 September 2006, https://www.hrw.org/news/2006/09/21/pakistan-free-kashmir-far-free. Accessed on 13 February 2024.

this serves as a clear indication that Azad Kashmir is not truly 'azad' as propagated by Pakistan.

In 1948, following the tribal raid and accession to the Indian Union, the J&K government promulgated the E&IMCO to control infiltration into the Valley from PoK and also unauthorized exit. This ordinance applied to the entire state, including areas under Pakistan's control. This ordinance is still in force as it was saved by the J&K Constitution and is now under the Jammu and Kashmir Reorganisation Act, 2019, along with the Enemy Agents Ordinance. Under section 2 of this ordinance, the government is empowered to 'order that any person for the time being in the state or any class of persons shall not proceed to a destination outside the state or move within the state from one place to another, except under the authority of a written permit'. Over the years, hundreds of people, including bona fide members of divided families visiting their relatives, were prosecuted and sentenced under the provisions of this draconian ordinance.

Section 21 of the ordinance even empowers the government to direct the removal from the Indian side of the CFL (now LoC) to the other side of the CFL (PoK) of any person who has committed or against whom reasonable suspicion exists that they have committed an offence under the ordinance. In common parlance, these powers came to be known as powers to push back in judicial and official records. Many times, even the courts would order the violator to be pushed back after they had undergone their sentence, regardless of whether the convict belonged to India or PoK.

A person to be pushed back is handed over to the SSP of Baramulla, who hands them over to the army at the appropriate level. The army would push back the person to the other side at a fixed point in the forward area of the Uri sector in the absence of any civil authority, police officer or magistrate. The fate of the persons so pushed back was unknown. Many times, such unfortunate people would get caught in hostile exchanges of fire, harmed by undetected mines laid on both sides of the CFL or LoC or even deliberately shot by the army of either side.

TEENAGE INFILTRATORS

I would like to narrate the story of two teenage boys, Sajad and Haneef, who had been arrested on suspicion of espionage after they crossed the CFL into the Uri sector. Suspicion was particularly strengthened because they had attempted to infiltrate on the day the Indo-Pak war of 1971 broke out, with the bombardment of Srinagar airport by the Pakistan Air Force. They allegedly possessed a bundle of printed posters advocating azadi. With a couple of years in jail pending investigation and trial, both were ordered to be pushed back in 1973. Accordingly, as per routine, Srinagar Police sent them to me to transfer them to the army. I was very much moved by their childlike, innocent faces when they were produced before me in handcuffs at the District Police Office, Baramulla. I couldn't speak for a while as I wondered about the fate awaiting these two teenagers at the LoC. Their survival while crossing was not guaranteed. With these thoughts troubling my mind, I directed them to be handed over to the SHO at the Baramulla Police Station till arrangements were finalized with the army. I faced the challenge of ensuring their safe crossing, of which the chances looked bleak. I don't know why their innocent faces haunted me even in my sleep—I wanted to ensure their safe crossing. But how I could ensure that was the big question troubling me and guiding my conscience. If they were handed over to the army, my conscience would not be satisfied as I would not be able to know about their safe passage. I decided to explore a way out.

I took up the matter with GOC 19 Division Major General S.C. Sinha, a noble officer with whom I had positive working relations. I had a feeling that the general would help without going into the routine modalities otherwise applicable to such cases. I strongly hoped that he would find a way out once I made him aware of my apprehensions. I called on him and briefed him regarding all the facts as well as my concerns. I requested him to find a way out for their safe crossing over into PoK. After hearing me, he put up his hands and told me there was no way to ensure their safety because the designated point for pushback had been determined at the LoC since the 1949 ceasefire and the army was neither responsible nor able to ensure that the person had crossed over to PoK safely. 'The borders being always volatile, I cannot ensure the safe crossing of the boys to the other side,' he clarified in no uncertain terms. As I knew the GOC's humanitarian feelings, I pressed him to find a way out. I told him that as persons in positions of authority, both of us were accountable to the Almighty if we acted routinely or mindlessly. In that process, two precious lives may be lost. I knew the terrain along the LoC like the back of my hand, so I had an idea that I wanted to share with the general.

I suggested that he could order their pushback via the Keran sector because according to my perception and considering the topography of that sector, they would not be out of sight till they were taken into custody by the army on the other side. He immediately rejected my suggestion. According to him, I was asking for something completely unprecedented and impossible; in the past, no one had been pushed back through Keran or any other sector besides the designated point in Uri. He further argued that the other side may even misunderstand such a pushback of two civilians and may open fire on them. Hammering my point further, I recommended a picket on the LoC in the Keran sector where the boys could be physically handed over to the Pakistani Army manning the picket on the opposite side. At that point, the two sides were are divided only by a narrow hilly nallah, which was usually dry. After much persuasion, he agreed.

Though there was an element of risk, I was mentally relieved and thanked him. It was decided that the two boys would be handed over to a mutually agreed Indian army post in Keran, where the LoC passed through the left bank of the Kishanganga (Neelum). The exchange between the two sides would occur at a stone's throw away from the LoC. I had visited this picket on our side during one of my visits to that area. From our side of the nallah, the Pakistani picket was within walkable distance, only a couple of yards away. Given the short distance, I had exchanged good wishes with the Pakistani boys manning the picket. Therefore, during the handover, the troops of both sides could communicate verbally with each other. This was why I had proposed this sector to the GOC. Accordingly, the boys were sent to Keran with a police escort, where they were physically handed over by the Indian Army to a Pakistani non-commissioned officer. However, before receiving the boys, the officer might have had to get clearance from their higher-up, which took some time. They crossed the dry nallah and stepped into PoK in full view of our police escort and Indian army soldiers. After receiving the boys, the Pakistani Army personnel put them in a jeep and drove them away. They smiled and waved to our army as well as to the police party from the jeep while traveling on the Athmuqam–Muzaffarabad road.

Upon his return, the inspector reported to me about their safe pushback. I was mentally and emotionally relieved and thanked the Almighty for giving me the strength and opportunity to execute this mission to my utmost satisfaction. I thank Major General (later Lieutenant General) S.C. Sinha, without whose positive approach and cooperation the mission could not have been accomplished.

Without his support, I could not have ensured the boys' safety. Later, I came to know from various travellers that the boys had happily joined their families. In the early 1980s, I also found out that Sajad was happily married and was running a music shop in Muzaffarabad. However, I did not get any updates about Haneef.

To my knowledge, this was the first and last pushback that was allowed to go through the Keran sector by the army. It was not a pushback but a formal handover and takeover between two friendly army units. Alas, this cordial relationship has been spoiled since 1988 when Pakistan began providing arms and training to Kashmiri youth to fight against India for azadi.

Though a small humanitarian gesture on the part of both armies, the governments of India and Pakistan could learn from this peace mission that was accomplished without any high-profile diplomatic or bureaucratic intervention. Only one Indian Army general, a police officer and an unknown Pakistani Army general, without whose knowledge our mission could not have been accomplished, were involved in this mission.

JOURNALIST'S PUSHBACK

This is the story of how a journalist was pushed back into the Valley for opposing the PoK establishment and for supporting azadi as the only solution to the Kashmir problem. The journalist is none other than late Khawaja Sanaullah Bhat. When I interviewed Yusuf Jameel, he said, 'Khawaja sahib didn't migrate to Pakistan as such. Prior to Partition, he had a canteen for the British Army at Calcutta. After Partition, he chose to return to Kashmir via Rawalpindi, but while in the newly carved out country, he got stuck there during the outbreak of the first Kashmir war towards the end of 1947, commonly known as the Kabaili Raid.' Muhammad Saeed Asad, in his book, notes, 'Thereafter, he started an Urdu weekly "Kashmir" in Muzaffarabad, which was believed to be supportive of an independent Kashmir. Eventually, troubles started for him, and he was pushed back to Jammu and Kashmir through the Poonch area of the CFL in the early 1950s.'[35] Once in this part of the state, he launched the weekly, which was soon turned into a daily.

In his book *Kashmiris Fight for Freedom*, Justice M.Y. Saraf of the Azad Kashmir Supreme Court provides the specific background that led to Sanaullah Bhat's pushback order. According to Saraf, the story was, 'A very unfortunate incident that happened when Sardar Qayyum was at the helm of affairs was the highly objectionable and arbitrary manner in which three Kashmiri political workers, Mr Sanaullah Bhat, Khawaja Amir-ud-Din and Wali Mohammad Aadil, were pushed across the CFL in the dead of the night.'[36] An interesting phase of Khawaja sahib's life, as described by Justice M.Y. Saraf, is as follows[37]:

> Mr Azizullah Hassan (Chief Secretary of PaK [sic]) had filed a private complaint u/s 500, Penal Code (Defamation) against Mr. Sanaullah Bhat, [...] Editor of a local weekly. The case arose out of a certain allegation levelled by the newspaper against Mr. Hassan in connection with loss of [...] carpet during the visit of Mr. Iskandar Mirza who paid an overnight visit to Muzaferabad [sic] while Sardar Qaiyum [sic] was in power.
>
> 'While the case was still pending, one dark night, the three persons mentioned earlier, together with Khawaja Habib Ullah Lone and Mr. Ghulam Rasool Sopori alias

[35]Asad, Muhammad Saeed, *Deewanon Pe Kya Guzri*, National Institute of Kashmir Studies, Mirpur, 2012, 25.

[36]Saraf, Muhammad Yusuf, *Kashmiris Fight for Freedom, Vol. 2 (1947–1978)*, Ferozsons, Pakistan, 1979, 1315.

[37]Ibid. 1314–16.

> Tara were arrested by the police on the night of 8th and 9th March and removed to Poonch; within [...] next two days the first three were pushed across the ceasefire line. Actually all the five were pre-partition political workers opposed to National Conference. In Muzaferabad they were playing the role of an opposition group and whenever a Central Minister, officer, a foreign journalist or guest paid a visit, they would meet him [sic] to air their views; generally they were critical of local administration. Those very days two members of the British Parliament, Mr. Bennet of Conservative Party and Mr. Stacey of Labor Party, visited Muzaferabad. They met them as usual and complained about India's failure to hold [...] plebiscite. It is claimed that they also told the members that in addition to the choice of accession to either Dominion, the people of Kashmir should have the option of independence [...] This highhanded step had been taken by Azizullah Hassan to escape the defamation case. But he is claimed to have secured a post-expulsion order in writing from the President that they be pushed back; he was led to believe that as Head of the State, he stood protected while civil servants had no escape.

Invariably, in those days, a pushed back person would be targeted and shot dead by the troops of either country while crossing the CFL, as there was no arrangement between the two countries of informing each other in advance about any civilian movement. If any individuals were lucky enough to survive, they were taken into custody by the army on the other side. After being interrogated by the army for as long as they wished, they would be handed over to the local police, sometimes even after months of their arrest. The local police, after questioning them, would hand them over to the SS at Srinagar, headed by Sheikh Ghulam

Qadir Ganderbali. The SS would take their own time to satisfy themselves about the bona fides of the person and prosecute them in the court under the provisions of the E&IMCO. It would take months or even years for the courts to decide whether the 'infiltrator' was to be pushed back after conviction. There was no separation of judiciary in the state. The state was the final authority in deciding whether an 'infiltrator' would be allowed to resettle in the state. Very few people were allowed to resettle in the Valley, that too only under the orders of Prime Minister Bakshi Ghulam Mohammad. Otherwise, the majority were pushed back after undergoing an imprisonment sentence ordered by the courts for offences under section 2/3 of E&IMCO. Khawaja sahib's case seems to have been dealt with differently.

Saraf further adds, 'A few days later, the MPs visited Srinagar where the three externees (whom they had met in PoK) met them again and told them how they had been pushed back. This became international news and put the Pakistani government in a very awkward position.'[38] Surprisingly, while recording important political events in his memoir, *Kashmir, 1947 to 1977*, Khawaja sahib is silent about the circumstances that led to his 'pushback' from PoK or his political or professional activities that led to his externment and rehabilitation in Srinagar. To the best of my knowledge, he has made no mention anywhere about how he got close to the powers that led to his rehabilitation in the Indian part of the state. He is also silent about how he established a daily newspaper. In those days, nobody could even dream of publishing a newspaper unless they were close to the person highest in power, just below Prime Minister Bakshi Ghulam Mohammad.

During my student days and thereafter, while strolling up and down Residency Road, Srinagar, with my friends, I would

---

[38]Ibid.

often see Khawaja sahib in the company of Sheikh Ghulam Qadir Ganderbali sahib near the Kothibagh headquarters of SS. The circumstances surely indicate that Ganderbali sahib was largely instrumental in his honourable rehabilitation because he wielded absolute powers as head of the SS directly under Prime Minister Bakshi Ghulam Mohammad. Ganderbali sahib had become more powerful, particularly after the dismissal and arrest of Sheikh Mohammad Abdullah.

Ganderbali sahib, a highly competent police officer, was successful in creating a very effective intelligence network to deal with subversive elements and opponents of the establishment. His initial rise to power immediately after 1948 is attributed to his one-time mentor, Peer Maqbool Geelani sahib, a very influential and venerated person of Kashmir and the chief mutawalli of the Astan-e-Aaliya of Sheikh Abdul Qadir Jilani (RUA) at Khanyar and Srinagar. It is believed that initially Peer Maqbool was responsible for projecting Ganderbali sahib as a capable officer immediately after the tribal attack. He rose from the lowest rank of head constable to that of a DIG and remained very active till Sadiq came to power in 1965. Maqbool Geelani was the emergency officer of Uri in Sheikh sahib's emergency administration after the 1947 tribal attack. In 1953, Peer sahib had reportedly gone underground, fearing arrest by Ganderbali sahib. Though close friends, both were afraid of each other after 1953. Later, Geelani was said to have received asylum from the PHC which arranged his incognito travel to Pakistan, where he ultimately died under circumstances not befitting a person of his ecclesiastical and political status.

Once when I was on tour with Ganderbali sahib as DIG Kashmir, he told me, 'I don't fear an attack on me from across the border except if it is sponsored by Peer Maqbool. Peer was resourceful enough to get me eliminated anywhere at his will.'

How ironic, I thought. During his illness, I used to visit him daily at the Jammu Dak Bungalow. Later, Bakshi Ghulam Mohammad had him shifted to All India Institute of Medical Sciences, New Delhi, for treatment, where he passed away.

Khawaja Sanaullah and Ganderbali sahib became great friends, though Khawaja sahib is silent on this topic in his writings. One thing is certain: without Ganderbali sahib's good wishes, Khawaja sahib could not have launched the weekly, *Aftab*, which was later converted into a daily. No person could even think of it without a nod from Prime Minister Bakshi Ghulam Mohammad. Khawaja sahib seems to have never forgotten his mentor Ganderbali sahib. I vividly recollect and state with full responsibility that he had prominently displayed a photograph of Ganderbali sahib on the wall of his office, just above his chair, with a bold caption, 'Quaid-e-Karvaan, Sheikh Ghulam Qadir'.

Initially, *Aftab* toed a cautious pro-establishment line, but later, with Sadiq's freedom of expression policies, Khawaja sahib would take the government to task on various social, administrative and political issues. Though Khawaja sahib was a fair and independent journalist, sometimes his personal interests would overcome his principles. He was short-tempered and would lose his cool at the drop of a hat. I have also been at the receiving end of his hot temper, but I too did not hesitate to reciprocate in kind, even during my deputy SP days.

Many times Khawaja sahib was unreasonable to the core. When he was barely in his twenties, Tahir Mohi-ud-Din, now a senior journalist of the state, was Khawaja sahib's blue-eyed boy. Even though he had many senior journalists working in his office, Khawaja sahib personally came to my office to get a no objection certificate to declare Tahir as the editor of the *Aftab*. At that time, I did not know Tahir, although he was from my home district. I asked Khawaja sahib, 'What is so special about this young man that you want to hand over the baton to him in your lifetime?' 'You don't know him. He is a journalist par excellence, a gem, and I want him to take over all my responsibilities and succeed me,' he replied emotionally. I issued the necessary certificate, and after some more formalities, Tahir was officially declared the editor of *Aftab*. It was really an honour for young Tahir to be an editor of a popular daily, that too at such a young age.

Shortly thereafter, I don't remember exactly after how long, Khawaja sahib rang me up and told me, or rather shouted at me, 'Tahir has cheated me. He has left. Arrest him immediately'. What I could gather from his shouting was that Tahir had resigned as editor of *Aftab* and joined *Aiena*, the newspaper founded by the late Shamim Ahmed Shamim. After his death, the paper was being run by his family under the patronage of Mohammad Syed Malik, his brother-in-law and a prominent journalist in his own right. I told Khawaja sahib sternly that it was not possible to arrest Tahir unless there was a proper written complaint against him for having committed a cognizable offence. 'Why do you need a report? The police have the power to arrest anybody', he replied, asserting his 'legal knowledge'. However, I insisted on a written report. 'I will send the report right away, but I want him arrested immediately,' he replied. I told him to send a report to the Miasuma Police Station near his office.

Later, the SHO informed me that Bhat had sent a report about Tahir having allegedly cheated some people by promising them government jobs. On the face of it, the allegation seemed to be concocted only to get Tahir arrested and to pressurize him to return to Khawaja sahib. However, in view of the written complaint, the SHO summoned Tahir to the police station, but Mohammad Syed Malik bailed him out immediately. Then, hell broke loose. Khawaja sahib rang me up again, spitting fire. 'How has Tahir been released even before his arrest?', he lost his temper and started threatening me. I tried explaining the legal position to him but he would not listen. Having no option, I hung up. We were not on talking terms for quite some time after the incident but eventually reconciled. Khawaja sahib had a strange love–hate relationship with me. We had several verbal duels on the phone over minor issues, but I never reacted to anything that he published against the police or against me in my professional capacity. That was our policy with every newspaper. Nevertheless, whenever we were face to face, he was always polite, courteous and respectful.

Khawaja sahib never left a stone unturned in his hospitality towards me at social gatherings organized by Sirajs, the trustees of *Aftab*. Lastly, I must say that he was a great journalist. Some of the present-day talented journalists, who had worked under his patronage, have reached great heights in their profession. Over time, *Aftab* became an institution with its independent policy. Because he had no family or children of his own, he had handed over all the rights of *Aftab* to a trust established by a prominent business house, Indo-Kashmir Carpet Company, led by the late Haji Mohammad Jamaal Siraj. The Sirajs were probably related to him because he would be worried whenever they faced any problem. Haji's son and a great friend of mine, Ghulam Mohammad Siraj, took a keen interest in maintaining the required standard of the paper even after Khawaja sahib passed away. May Allah grant Janatul Firdous to Khawaja Sanaullah Bhat sahib. He will always be remembered as a pioneer of modern journalism in the state.

Chapter 5

Ominous Vibes

SERIAL BOMBING

Before December 1983, a series of bomb explosions rocked the office of the Urdu daily *Srinagar Times* at Budshah Chowk, India Coffee House on Residency Road, Bakshi Stadium during the Independence Day parade and the residence of Justice A.S. Anand, a serving judge of the J&K High Court (later elevated to Chief Justice of India). Though these explosions did not cause any major damage, injury or death of any person, they were enough to instil fear and panic among the general populace. The overall situation in the Valley was also very disturbing, with youths and students always on the lookout to create disturbances on one pretext or the other.

During this chaotic situation, a One Day International cricket match was organized on 13 October 1983 at the Sher-e-Kashmir Cricket Stadium, Srinagar, between India and West Indies. The match caused great embarrassment to the central and state governments when the spectators converted the match into a massive anti-India demonstration. The spectators openly expressed hostility towards Indian players and subjected them to the worst type of heckling and dirty abuses in the presence of some of their families. The rival West Indies team was cheered and encouraged. Nonstop pro-Pakistan, pro-azadi and anti-India slogans were raised. It was a free for all wherein the police were silent spectators who did not intervene at all. Even all the senior officers of the police and paramilitary forces deployed there were watching helplessly. Finally, the unruly spectators attempted to dig up the pitch. I was observing this spectacle from the official gallery as I was not in any manner associated with law and order.

CM Farooq Abdullah could only watch helplessly as the scene unfold. As a result of this event, he became the target of severe criticism by the Congress party at the Centre; they had already been after him. Indira Gandhi and her cronies in the state were always on the lookout for an opportunity to dismiss Farooq sahib and destabilize the state to grab power. Such conspiracies hatched by the central and state leadership of the Congress party coupled with violent activities by resistance groups added disturbing dimensions to the state of affairs. The Congress government at the Centre, instead of strengthening the Farooq government in national interest, always pursued their party agenda at the cost of destabilizing the sensitive state.

Analysing the embarrassing situation created during the cricket match in Srinagar, one wonders how this international event was unprecedentedly decided to be held in Srinagar for the first time by the Board of Control for Cricket in India. It was not part of any series but an unscheduled friendly match. Were the intelligence agencies aware of the possible repercussions? To me, this seems like a plan hatched by the Congress government to catch Farooq sahib on the wrong foot and create an adverse public opinion against him in the country to justify his removal.

In this chaotic situation, the investigation was handed to me in December 1983. Naturally, my first priority was to look into the serial bombing, which had been investigated in only a routine manner by the concerned police, who appeared clueless. I was still trying to investigate the matter, when, to my shock, on 29 March 1984, an explosion occurred at Nagbal, Anantnag, a highly revered religious place of the Kashmiri Pandits. Thanks to traditional brotherhood and communal amity between Muslims and the Kashmiri Pandits, the situation remained peaceful. The Nagbal blast was obviously aimed at disturbing communal peace in the state. Another bomb ripped apart the wall of the office chambers of Ale Ahmad Suroor, the head of the Iqbal Institute at Kashmir University and a very eminent scholar. He had a providential escape as he and some of his colleagues had left the room seconds before. This explosion created a lot of panic and sent shock waves across the campus. This was the first time that a prestigious seat of learning had been targeted. Two other bombs were thrown, one at the house of Neelkanth Ganjoo, a judge at Karan Nagar, Srinagar, who had sentenced Maqbool Bhat to death, while the other targeted a state transport corporation bus in Sopore on 26 April 1984.

To give serious thought and proper direction to the investigation, the DGP convened a meeting of all concerned officers, including officers of the CID Special Branch and CI. Very upset about the repeated blasts at different places in the Valley, he ordered the formation of a joint SS of the CID, CI and regular police to exclusively investigate all cases of serial bombings by pooling all available resources.

Many suspects were questioned by the CI with no fruitful result. Suddenly, after a few days, the SP CI called and asked me to urgently join him at the JIC as there had been an important breakthrough. When I joined him, he was quizzing a young man named Fida, a salesman at the Government Arts Emporium. The SP asked the young man to tell me what all he had disclosed to him. Fida, without any hesitation stated:

'Sir, a few years ago I was posted as salesman at the J&K Government Arts Emporium on Prithviraj Road, New Delhi.

Besides domestic customers, many foreigners and diplomats routinely came to shop for Kashmir handicrafts, such as handwoven carpets, exquisite shawls, wood carving and papier-mâché. Some PHC diplomats were also our customers. With their frequent visits, some of them developed quite an intimate relationship with me. At times, they would take me out for a cup of tea or even a meal. As our relationship matured, they confided in me and asked me to work for them in Kashmir. Explaining their plan of subversion and sabotage, they also motivated me to help create an underground organizational set-up for such covert activities. After I agreed to take up the assignment, they told me that I would have to visit Dubai with them to meet some important Pakistani dignitary for further instructions. I readily accepted their offer, and on the fixed date, I travelled with one of them to Dubai, where I was made comfortable in a hotel. After a couple of days, I was taken to a five-star hotel, where I was surprised to see General Zia-ul-Haq, the president of Pakistan, when I was ushered into his suite. I was introduced to him, and he welcomed me profusely. He questioned me about my profession and the situation in the Valley. Though I was very nervous, I told him whatever I could. He seemed impressed. Ultimately, Zia-ul-Haq told me that he was very pleased with my zeal and willingness to work for Pakistan. On returning to Delhi, I was trained by Pakistanis in assembling crude bombs with locally available material, such as potassium chlorate and arsenic sulphate. After a few months, I was transferred to Srinagar, but I did not pursue the assignment further.'

After hearing Fida, we decided to dissect his statement to arrive at the truth and not jump to any conclusion. It sounded unreal that the president of Pakistan met a freshly recruited, low-level ISI operative. He had foolishly tried to impress us by name dropping. For us, the positive takeaway of his story was his clean admission of being an ISI agent trained in assembling crude bombs to organize and oversee acts of sabotage and subversion in the Valley. With his own admission of being a highly motivated and committed Pakistani secret agent, the needle of suspicion conclusively pointed towards him as the kingpin of the serial blasts in the Valley. After being trained as a bomb maker, why would he leave his mission unfinished or give up his assignment for no reason? Incidentally, the serial bombing incidents coincided with Fida's transfer to Srinagar. Therefore, we decided to treat him as a prime suspect to be professionally quizzed further to draw out the whole truth. He had cleverly avoided mentioning the serial bomb blasts in the Valley. 'This salesman is concealing the active phase of his mission, and I guess he is yet to divulge the full story,' I told my colleague.

Accordingly, Fida was questioned again in a sustained and methodical manner by the CI staff, who confronted him with his own admissions. By evening, he started spilling the beans. He stated that after he was transferred to Srinagar, he formed a group of about 10 trusted boys whom he trained in assembling and using low-grade crude bombs made from locally available chemicals and components. He admitted that his boys had caused the blasts with such locally made devices at various places in Srinagar and its suburbs. He further disclosed that a senior separatist underground leader, Shabir Shah, was in the loop because he was given the impression that the boys were working on behalf of his organization. Fida would voluntarily report to him after every explosion.

The alarming part of his statement was the disclosure regarding the involvement of two youths: one, the son of a senior SP (later DIG) and the other, the son of an IAS officer who headed the most sensitive departments in the state, including the home department and internal security. Although the parents were unaware of their sons' subversive activities, the raids conducted at their residences confirmed that the serial bombings had been carried out by the group under Fida's leadership. All the boys, including the officers' sons, involved in assembling bombs and conducting the blasts were picked up. All of them individually admitted what the salesman—their boss—had disclosed. The whole group was arrested, and some live crude bombs and components, including potassium nitrate and potassium chlorite, were seized from their possession.

Shabir Shah, their self-styled underground patron, was also arrested from his rented house. After his arrest, an unobtrusive trap was laid at his residence to pick up and question his contacts who were likely to visit his house. The day after his arrest, a young girl from the neighbourhood entered the house and was apprehended. When the officer in charge of the trap informed me about the identity of the girl, I told him to quiz her on the spot and that if he was convinced about her lack of involvement in the blasts, to quietly escort her to her parent's house without arousing the suspicion of the people residing in the area. She belonged to a respectable family, and her father, a senior government officer, and her uncle were very well known to me. I was personally convinced that the poor girl was not involved in any subversive activities. Her family's dignity and honour were protected. The leader, however, was detained.

With the arrest of the senior officers' sons, a notorious propaganda machine was unleashed against my colleagues and I. The parents accused us of having 'framed' their sons. Nevertheless, we proceeded with the case undeterred and in a fair manner. However, after being kept under detention for some time and counselled properly, the boys were released and rehabilitated like every other member of the secret cell. Both the young men and their associates are well settled in their respective businesses.

CYCLOSTYLE MACHINE THEFT

Underground groups kept cropping up after the wiping out of Al Fatah, the formidable guerrilla organization. A report was lodged by Government Medical College (GMC) authorities at the Karan Nagar Police Station, Srinagar, about the theft of a cyclostyle machine from the first floor of the college building. The investigating officer (IO) initiated a routine investigation to trace the crime and the culprits. However, nothing was found. Typically, the theft of a cyclostyle machine would not be a big deal to worry about. As a supervisory officer, I did not take special interest in the case either as, I was busy with more important matters.

Sometime after the theft, while discussing this case in a routine meeting to review the crime situation, the IO told me, 'Sir, a spot inspection of the crime scene does not indicate a burglary, as everything, including the doors and windows of the room with inner bolts, is intact. There are no marks of any possible weapon having been used to break open a door or window to gain access. Sir, there is nothing to show that it is an outsider's job.' 'What do you mean? Do you think it is the work of one of the office hands who may have removed the machine to sell it and that the burglary story has been cooked up to cover the crime?' I asked. 'Sir, I can't say with certainty, but it is clear that the room has not been broken into. It has not been accessed from the outside,' he replied.

Suddenly, the Red Kashmir cyclostyled posters from the 1960s flashed in my mind. I wondered if it could be an operation of some unknown underground outfit. To clear my doubts, I decided to personally inspect the crime scene. Upon visiting the place, I concluded that the IO may be right. Therefore, my suspicion turned to the staff, as there was no sign to suggest that any outsider had broken into the room. I put some other officers on duty to probe the subversive angle of the story. They were instructed to use all their secret resources to find out the truth. My idea of investigating the Red Kashmir angle paid off because it caused quite a bit of panic among some youth groups. In a few days, an asset asked me to question some teenage boys whom he named. When asked for further details, he told me that some 9th- and 10th-grade students of a nearby school were suspected to have committed this theft. Their recent behaviour and movements had been suspicious, and they had been seen meeting in isolated places. Besides, they were maintaining some distance from other schoolmates. I asked the IO to pick up the suspected boys by taking their parents into confidence because otherwise they were likely to go underground. I also instructed him not to keep them in a lockup as that may have a negative psychological impact on them.

Four boys were produced before me the next day at the Kothibagh Police Station. Seeing their innocent faces with not even a strand of a beard, I was sceptical about their involvement. How could these innocent-looking children commit such a crime without leaving a trace? I called one of the boys, Farooq Renzu, the son of a policeman (who was earlier an active member of Ganderbali sahib's Special Staff), into a room. I made him comfortable and talked to him about his studies and other matters a boy of his age would be interested in. Once he relaxed, I asked him, 'Have you ever seen a machine that makes many copies of written papers?' He kept quiet and gazed at the floor. I repeatedly asked him the same question in different ways till he broke down and started crying. I got up and consoled him. Farooq confessed everything.

One by one, all four boys confessed that they had formed a secret cell of their own to circulate pro-azadi and anti-India posters. To facilitate their operations, they decided to steal a cyclostyle machine from some government office; the idea was given by one of the senior boys. For several days, they visited many government offices in the vicinity but did not find any such machine. Ultimately, they found one in an office room on the first floor of the GMC. How they had removed the machine from the room without leaving a clue was the million-dollar question. They had no accomplice within the GMC who could have acted as a collaborator and handed over the machine to them.

A hair-raising, innovative modus operandi was adopted by them to commit the crime. Farooq Renzu said, 'Sir, during our quest to find a cyclostyle machine to make copies of anti-India posters, we located one machine in the GMC office. We immediately decided to take it away during the night. We went there late at night. The chowkidar was asleep. We scaled the boundary wall and arrived in front of the main building without much effort. We could easily locate our target in the first floor room while standing in front of the building, as we had recced it earlier. Climbing on each other's backs, two of us landed on the concrete cantilever of the first floor, which was exactly outside the window of the room where we had seen the machine. The window was bolted from the inside. However, the black tin exhaust pipe of the stove (bukhari—used in winter to keep the room warm) was protruding out of a round tin plate hole fixed in the widow instead of a glass pane. Gently pushing the pipe inwards to enable us to put a hand through the round opening, one of us unbolted the window and opened it. Two of us entered the room through the window and tied the machine to a rope that we had carried with us. We slowly released the rope to slide the machine down through the window and over the cantilever. Once the machine touched the ground, it was untied by the other boys waiting in the lawn. Both of us came through the window, landed on the cantilever, closed the window, put our hand through the hole and bolted it again. The stove exhaust pipe was neatly pulled out through the hole in the tin plate.'

'What a neat operation, and what an effort to leave no trace of the crime!', my colleagues and I wondered. Nobody could even imagine that the stove pipe had ever been removed. Farooq continued, 'We jumped to the ground, and all of us left with the machine. Initially, we hid the machine in a local mosque but later removed it from there. As we had no place to conceal it, we threw it in the night soil of a public latrine near Gurgari Mohalla in downtown Srinagar. We planned on retrieving it later when the incident was forgotten'. All the four boys were quizzed separately, and they all confirmed the story. The machine was recovered by the police from under heaps of night soil in the public latrine.

On further questioning, they told the police that they committed the theft to arrange a valuable asset for the freedom struggle. They thought that the machine would be very useful in printing anti-India posters, which they intended to publish regularly. I wondered how it dawned on these youth to form their own outfit. They wanted to be collaborators of the resistance and contribute whatever they could by stealing the machine to print subversive material.

Ultimately, we decided to allow them to carry on with their studies and rehabilitated them, particularly in view of the cooperation of their parents and some influential persons of the locality. After a few days of police custody, they were released. None of them went down that path ever again. They completed their studies and succeeded in building their careers. Farooq Renzu joined the information department and climbed to the top. He retired as a head of the department. Another boy, Shah Din, joined the police department as a sub-inspector and retired as an SP. I am not sure what the other two did; they probably became businessmen. None of them thought of joining any subversive outfit again.

DUSSEHRA BOMBING PLAN

In 1984, a clandestine group was formed by Mahmood Sagar and Mustaq Sagar, two brothers from a Maharaja Bazar family. They were ideologically pro-Pakistan in terms of committing acts of subversion and sabotage. Their father, Mohammad Ismail Sagar, was an active member of the J&K Muslim Conference. The Sagar brothers were often part of one or the other covert and overt resistance groups. One of our assets was an insider of their group. He informed us about their dangerous plan of blasting bombs during the Dussehra celebrations at Hazuri Bagh (Iqbal Park), where traditionally thousands of spectators of all faiths watch the burning of Ravan's effigy. According to him, the group was in the process of assembling a few crude bombs for this purpose. We worked on this information methodically and an operation was planned with the insider's assistance. To swoop in on the entire group, we instructed our asset to arrange a meeting of all the members of the group along with explosives at Odeon Hotel on Residency Road, which is situated next door to the Kothibagh Police Station. Our covert operation was planned for one day before Dussehra. As planned, our asset would gather all the group members in the hotel room for a briefing and the distribution of explosives for the attack. We booked the hotel room under a false name. All of them, including the Sagar brothers, who were the brains behind this dangerous mission, came to the hotel room with the bombs to be distributed to the members for the attack the next day. They must have hardly taken their seats when a police party, in a clean operation, swooped into the room and apprehended all of them with all the crude bombs. No one in the busy market of Residency Road or even the hotel management found out about the operation. Simply recalling the dangerous designs of the members makes me shudder. Had they succeeded in this misadventure, innocent spectators would have died and scores more would have been injured. Many, particularly women and children, would have been victims of a stampede. Moreover, communal harmony would have been seriously affected.

In January 1990, when the LoC was thrown open, Mahmood Sagar crossed into PoK where he is said to have become an important member of the PoK chapter of the Hurriyat Conference. However, his younger brother is now a prominent trader representing various trade bodies in the Valley, apparently with no interest in separatist politics.

MARTYRS' DAY PROCESSION

After the Indira–Sheikh Accord of 1975, the situation in the Valley remained largely peaceful. The ISI also did not initiate any major subversive activity due to Sheikh Mohammad Abdullah's popularity. The ISI discouraged the Kashmiri youth whenever they sought arms from them. Instead, they encouraged them to strengthen home-grown resistance with local resources. They probably had adopted a policy of wait and watch. However, the dismissal of Farooq Abdullah's government on 2 July 1984 by Governor Jagmohan as per Mrs Gandhi's instructions boosted Farooq's popularity. The public was angry and worked up. To express their anger, they started contemplating planning an armed revolt against the Indian state, which would have been a disaster and ended in a bloodbath. Large contingents of paramilitary troops had been airlifted by Governor Jagmohan even before Farooq's formal removal, which was against all norms of federalism. Post dismissal, Farooq warned his party against any misconduct and advised them to be peaceful. Though out of power, he was against any bloodshed. As part of my duty to ensure peace and order, I remained in touch with him even after his dismissal. During one meeting, he confided in me that he would not like his people to rise in revolt against his unconstitutional dismissal and get killed. However, having lost faith in democracy, there were ominous vibes of renewed attempts of sabotage, subversion and armed revolt by the disenchanted youth.

However, on 13 July, which is Martyr's Day, provoked by Indian leaders like George Fernandes, Farooq attempted to take out the traditional procession from Mujahid Manzil, violating the curfew imposed in the city. Divisional Commissioner Hamidullah Khan, DC Ghulam Qadir Pardesi and I rushed and stopped him at Dalal Mohalla, hardly 50 yards from his party headquarters. He heeded our advice and called off the programme on our assurance that he would be allowed to take out the procession after receiving proper permission from the district magistrate. He was later accommodated, and the procession took place on 17 July with unprecedented participation from the people. No anti-national or anti-government slogans were raised. Mirwaiz Moulana Mohammad Farooq and Abdul Ghani Lone also participated. Winding its way through the narrow streets of downtown Srinagar with no special deployment of the police en route, the procession concluded peacefully at Martyrs' Graveyard on the premises of the Naqshband Sahab shrine. All the three leaders delivered speeches and paid homage to the martyrs. Nothing untoward happened.

Around the same time in the early 1980s, Shabir Shah, the senior separatist leader imprisoned in Tihar Jail, allegedly sent three of his senior associates with training facilities and funds to secure arms aid from the ISI to initiate an armed struggle against India. Pleading with the authorities there, they argued that the situation was ripe for an armed revolt in the Valley. The ISI officers refused to oblige them for unknown reasons. However, while discussing the Kashmir situation, the ISI officers allegedly expressed their dislike for Dr Farooq Abdullah, Mirwaiz Moulana Farooq and Abdul Ghani Lone—the three Kashmir-based senior leaders. Shabir's trio returned after they suspected that the ISI intended to play a bigger game.

CI sources later revealed that they had reliable information regarding plans for large-scale violence, disturbances, sabotage and subversion, particularly at the Martyrs' Graveyard, by a group of youth belonging to the NC and headed by one Farooq Khushu. CI officers had suspected that Khushu had the blessings of the ISI and that he and his associates were even assigned with the task of assassinating the three leaders. They believe that the timely intervention of the police and NC workers pushed back the crowd that had converged near the stage, potentially blowing the cover for possible assassins. The officers further claimed that a newly formed underground organization, Al Maqbool Muslim Mujahideen, had been commissioned by the ISI to assassinate the three leaders. It was believed that Mushtaq Zargar, aka Latram, was part of the group. However, I did not believe this story. As per my experience, the ISI would not trust such nonentities with an assassination mission and leave it to chance.

According to CI sources, Al Jihad, another small underground organization, surfaced around 1983–84 and was subsequently busted by them. According to them, this organization was responsible for publishing a four-page cyclostyled tract propagating jihad for the liberation of J&K. The pamphlet, which created quite a stir in the Valley, was printed on a crudely assembled cyclostyle machine.

Later, another subversive organization, Holy War Fighters,

emerged. These were the ominous beginnings of a bigger armed militancy operation in 1988. By that time, the trajectory of armed resistance had ascended to a much higher point; an arms cache had also been discovered in Rajouri by CI sleuths. In addition, a large number of arms was seized during the same period from other places.

LEST WE FORGET

An engraving on a marble slab outside the Martyrs' Graveyard at Bijbehara in south Kashmir is a blood-curdling and gory reminder of the killing of unarmed civilians by security forces on the national highway on 24 October 1993. The security forces, deployed in bulk to quell the uprising, felt free to kill as many people as they could in the absence of an effective civil administration during the governor's rule. The Bijbehara incident of 24 October 1993, narrated by a survivor named Reyaz Ahmed Ganai, which is available on social media, is quoted as an example of many such bloody incidents. Reyaz recounts that when he was in eighth grade, he was part of a large but peaceful slogan-shouting procession of about 20,000 people that was taken out in the town. They were peacefully proceeding on the highway when Reyaz heard gunfire. As he attempted to run away, one procession member caught hold of him and did not let him go. Reyaz was accompanied by Kamal ji, a Kashmiri Pandit boy who was his friend and cricket playmate. Just then, the BSF started firing indiscriminately, and Reyaz saw people falling on the road. As soon the firing subsided, Reyaz got up but was fired upon. Kamal ji was also fired upon and died on the spot. Reyaz says he felt his intestines coming out. He was rushed to the local hospital where he was made to wait because the doctors prioritized treating those who were deemed to have a higher chance of survival. They believed that Reyaz was a hopeless case and would not survive, so that time was allocated to other patients. However, after treating the rest of the injured, they also operate upon Reyaz. Miraculously, he lived to tell the story! According to him, all the injured, who had been given preferential care by the doctors, died. This is perhaps the only incident in which a Kashmiri Pandit boy was killed by security forces while participating a peaceful procession.

Chapter 6

Big Games

Since 1947, the common people of J&K, particularly those of the Valley, have been victims of big games played by various powers to deprive them of their basic rights. Pakistan too has always tried to destabilize the state through covert war. Though the volume of these big games is very large, I have only briefly made some of them a part of this project to make my readers aware of what all had been happening behind the curtain.

TRIBAL ATTACK

Despite Maharaja Hari Singh, the ruler of J&K state, having a standstill agreement with Pakistan, in 1947 Pakistan played a big game by launching a surprise tribal attack on the state in October under the overall command of their army officers. The maharaja was pushed to sign the Instrument of Accession with the Indian Union, wherein he conceded only the three subjects of defence, external affairs and communications to the Centre. This was on the condition that the will of the people would be ascertained once peace was restored. Under these circumstances, neither Maharaja Hari Singh nor Sheikh Mohammad Abdullah, the chief minister of the state, was left with any other option, though both aspired for an independent state with the maharaja as its titular head. Interestingly, on more than one occasion, Nehru had stuck to the same line and made repeated commitments to ascertain the will of the people regarding accession of the state.[39] Pakistan's rash and untimely action pushed the state into a perpetual firestorm, thereby resulting in death and destruction that continues till this day.

SHEIKH ABDULLAH ARRESTED

On 9 August 1953, the then prime minister of India, Jawaharlal Nehru, played a big game when he ordered the dismissal of Sheikh Mohammad Abdullah, the prime minister of J&K, thus destabilizing the state. With this unwarranted action, the separatist movement established its roots when Mirza Afzal Beg formed the PF under the patronage of Sheikh Abdullah. The PF demanded the implementation of the UNSC resolution to ascertain the will of the people.

BAKSHI REMOVED

Subsequently, Jawaharlal Nehru sought the resignation of Bakshi Ghulam Mohammad, his puppet prime minister, in 1964, exercising what is known as the Kamaraj Plan. Though Nehru wanted G.M. Sadiq to succeed him, Bakshi manipulated him to get the oath of office administered to his puppet, Shamas-ud-Din, an insignificant and unimpressive minister in his cabinet. Ultimately, Nehru's will prevailed and Sadiq was sworn in in 1965. A leftist to the core, he allowed Article 370 to be eroded by rendering it ineffective except in terms of safeguarding jobs and seats in professional colleges for state citizens only. He also converted Sheikh's NC into the All India National Congress and downgraded the status and powers of an elected Sadar-i-Riyasat by placing the governor as the head

---

[39]Watali, Ali M., *Kashmir Intifada*, Gulshan Books, Srinagar, 2017, 222.

of the state as in other states. All these schemes contributed to the expansion of the separatist movement with the formation of violent underground cells.

OPERATION GIBRALTAR

In August 1965, after the tribal raid fiasco of 1947, Pakistan launched Operation Gibraltar by pushing regular troops into the state in plain clothes and armed with lethal weaponry. Although Operation Gibraltar failed and resulted in the Indo-Pak war of 1965, the Kashmiri youth were inspired by the infiltrating Mujahideen. More underground cells were formed as the youth sought arms. Several bomb blasts were conducted by underground activists using the infiltrators' leftover explosives. As the first militant attack in the Valley, one such underground outfit stabbed and killed Constable Charan Dass of the BSF on 3 February 1966.

MRS GANDHI'S GAMES

With Sheikh sahib behind bars, puppet governments were foisted upon the state from 1953 to 1975 by Nehru and later his daughter, Mrs Indira Gandhi, without any credible election process. Even after the Indira–Sheikh Accord of 1975, Mrs Gandhi in 1997; she propped up Mufti Sayed as the CM. Sheikh Mohammad Abdullah, who was in power with Congress support, acted fast and recommended fresh elections under governor's rule. Sheikh won with two-thirds majority in all the three regions of the state, hence making not only the Congress and ruling Janata Party eat dust but also defeating communal parties like the JI and Jana Sangh.

SUCCESSION GAME

On Mrs Gandhi's advice, in his lifetime Sheikh Abdullah nominated Dr Farooq as his successor, but on the eve of his death, she prevented him from taking the oath of office. The Congress party attempted to reverse the process initiated with the Indira–Abdullah Sheikh of 1975. Though Dr Farooq enjoyed two-thirds majority in the state assembly, Mrs Gandhi attempted to resume power surrendered by her to Sheikh in 1975. Though seriously ill, Sheikh was still alive when a fake intelligence report was fed to me about the plan of some Kashmiri youth to forcibly take over Sheikh's coffin and bury him covered in the Pakistani flag. Another fake intelligence report mentioned the possible outbreak of communal riots soon after the doyen's death was made public. The army's subarea commander, without any request from the district administration, offered me army assistance for advance deployment in the city's police stations. From the above incidents, I surmised that this was part of the Congress's multi-pronged plan to secure power in the state. Without believing these fake intelligence reports, I, as the SSP, made foolproof arrangements in advance for crowd control as lakhs of grief-stricken people were expected to converge in Srinagar for their leader's funeral.

RAJ BHAVAN DRAMA

I was a witness to the actual drama that unfolded at Raj Bhavan. Immediately after Sheikh's death, Dr Farooq, along with a few of his party colleagues, approached me and asked me to accompany them. As we reached Raj Bhavan, Dr Farooq and his group marched straight into a huge drawing room where two of his ministers, Devi Das Thakur and G.M. Bhaderwahi, were already present with Governor B.K. Nehru. Thakur and the governor were enjoying a drink. Dr Farooq asked the governor to administer the oath of office to him. The governor hesitated on some pretext. It seemed that he was waiting for directions from Delhi. Meanwhile, party general secretary Ghulam Mohi-ud-Din Shah requested the governor to administer the oath to Dr Farooq as he had already been elected as the leader of the NC parliamentary party. Wasting an hour or so in unnecessary discussions, correcting and retyping errors in the oath document, the governor ultimately administered the oath of office to Dr Farooq.

I state with complete responsibility that had Dr Farooq not been administered the oath overnight or some other person like D.D. Thakur been declared as a caretaker chief minister, the state, particularly the volatile Valley, would have turned upside down with violent uprisings. In his autobiography, B.K. Nehru has narrated all these facts with some variations. However, he writes that he had later received a phone call from the prime minister's aide, Makhan Lal Fotedar, telling him that had he waited, Kashmir's history would have been different. The state would have undoubtedly ended up in a bloodbath.

ARSON GAME

Neither Mrs Gandhi nor her followers accepted Dr Farooq as chief minister. Thereafter, it was a free-for-all to play different games to remove him from power. On 19 May 1983, locals set the Congress office on fire. However, with the immediate intervention of fire services, no damage was caused. Supported by the national and local print media, the Congress party blamed Dr Farooq and his party workers for the arson. The game was, however, subsequently exposed by veteran journalist Arun Shourie in his investigative report published in *India Today* on 31 July 1983. The report was supported by photographic evidence obtained by him from some local press photographers.

ARMY ATTACKS CIVILIANS

The last nail in the coffin of political instability was an unprovoked attack by an errant group of the Indian army transport unit on unarmed civilians in Srinagar on 26 July 1980, over a minor accident with an auto rickshaw. Two civilians were killed, and numerous vehicles worth billions were damaged and burnt by the army in the Civil Lines area spanning from Batmaloo to Nehru Park, covering about 4 km. Despite being in uniform, I too was attacked and almost killed while rescuing a teenage boy from a rampaging army group. I managed to survive after I was left unconscious on the road. My colleagues were also injured in this senseless orgy of death and destruction.

The next day, rumours of my death in the hospital provoked a civilian uprising in the city. If not for Sheikh Mohammad Abdullah's timely intervention, the situation would have deteriorated beyond redemption. He rushed to Lal Chowk, the main city centre, climbed atop a bus and addressed the agitating crowd. His address cooled their tempers when he informed them that I was very much alive and out of danger. Thereafter, Sheikh sahib directly drove to Shri Maharaja Hari Singh Hospital to ask after me. He cheered me up by narrating incidents from his own life when he had received serious injuries during the freedom struggle. However, the damage was done. This ghastly incident wounded the psyche of the people, most of whom had tacitly accepted the status quo following the Indira–Sheikh Accord of 1975 that guaranteed autonomy. The massive mandate given to Sheikh Mohammad Abdullah in the 1977 elections was indicative of the majority support to the accord. The army attack on unarmed civilians in 1980 unfortunately reinforced the resolve of the Kashmiri youth to pick up arms against the state. The youth were already very keen to pick up arms after the failure of Operation Gibraltar in 1965 but this attack further strengthened their resolve.

FATAL ALLIANCE

After the unconstitutional dismissal of Dr Farooq by Jagmohan at the insistence of Indira Gandhi, her son, Prime Minister Rajiv Gandhi, restored power to Dr Farooq. This was part of a long-term game of a fatal pre-electoral alliance between the two parties at the Congress's behest. It was a Himalayan blunder as the alleged rigging of the 1987 elections served as the trigger for the Kashmiri youth to finally pick up arms.

RIGGING BOSS

After the 1987 pre-electoral alliance, I was summoned to Dr Farooq's residence where Rajesh Pilot, the union minister, and Ghulam Rasool Kar, a senior Congress leader, were already present. When asked for my assessment, I frankly told them that the Congress was not going to win any seat in the Valley. Later, a senior Congress leader called me for a midnight meeting at Broadway Hotel where she offered me a big suitcase filled with money to make them win the Anantnag assembly seat. I told her it was not possible and left. Later, Anantnag District SP Javed Makhdoomi informed me that another senior Congress minister had offered him money and promised him appointment as the DIG of railways. However, he did not succeed in winning him over.

Meanwhile, Dr Farooq was called to Delhi where intelligence agencies were used to tell him that he was losing 20 seats. Upon his return, during a meeting of senior officers, I assured him that in a free and fair election, his party was not going to lose more than 10 seats, which might go to the Muslim United Front (MUF). This was a game played by the Congress to make him panic and rig the elections. Satisfied with our assessment, Dr Farooq assigned the responsibility of briefing returning officers (ROs) to me and Financial Commissioner Hamidullah Khan to ensure that free and fair election were conducted. To facilitate quick action, he placed his helicopter at our disposal.

When the results were declared, the NC got the majority. However, the counting for the Anantnag seat was repeatedly deferred because of the ruckus created by Congress workers inside the hall. Furthermore, the situation in the town and suburbs was highly explosive. An *India Today* correspondent, who had returned from a south Kashmir tour, informed Dr Farooq about the volatile situation in Anantnag. He deputed me and Divisional Commissioner G.Q. Lone to get the counting expedited. Ghulam Hassan Shah, the RO, was called to the SSP's house to brief him about expediting the counting process. With some hesitation, he stated that he was being pressurized by the principal private secretary (PPS) to the CM to announce the result in favour of the Congress candidate. The PPS was misusing his position and rigging the election in favour of the Congress party to secure post-retirement extension of his career, which he actually achieved with his appointment as vice chancellor of a university. Despite the CM being ignorant about his misdeeds, his name was dragged into the public domain for being party to the rigging. It was later revealed that throughout the state, the PPS had got his favoured officers appointed as ROs, particularly in the constituencies where the Congress had won. With our intervention, the results were announced while we were there. The MUF candidate Sayed Shah, the brother of Shabir Shah, was declared the winning candidate for the Anantnag seat. In all, of the 10 seats that I had forecasted, the MUF won five seats, with the remaining five being won by NC candidates because of strong local influence on the ROs. I believe that except the PPS and his chosen lot, Dr Farooq or his officers were never a party to any rigging.

LONE-ZIA CONSPIRACY

Amidst this situation in the Valley, Zia-ul-Haq, the military dictator of Pakistan, decided to play a bigger game by providing arms to the Kashmiri youth in 1988. Abdul Ghani Lone, who was in London at the time, was called by the ISI and asked to come to Pakistan. As a precaution, he was advised to first fly to Tehran, where a Pakistani plane would be waiting to bring him to Karachi. A sitting minister, who was another ISI asset, was also summoned for the crucial meeting. Though Zia's game was for Pakistan to annex the state, Abdul Ghani Lone insisted on azadi. With his own hidden agenda, Zia accepted azadi as an objective. Thereafter, in pursuance of the covert alliance of General Zia-ul-Haq with Abdul Ghani Lone—who had revealed all these facts to me just before his assassination—and the sitting minister, the Kashmiri youth were provided training and arms to fight the Indian forces.

However, this tragic alliance failed to achieve its goals and instead caused an unprecedented annihilation of the Kashmiri youth. Because of this erroneous and deceptive alliance, Kashmir lost everything, including its state and basic democratic rights. It is time that we Kashmiris admit that the blood of innocent Kashmiris was shed in vain. The GoI will be well advised to reconsider their policy and announce a ceasefire to rehabilitate the gun-wielding Kashmiri youth.

FIRST MILITANT ATTACK

Militancy surfaced in the Valley with an attack on my Rajbagh residence in Srinagar on the night of 18 September 1988. One of the attackers was killed by the bullets of his own colleagues, which had actually been aimed at my security guard at the gate, who was hit by a bullet in his thigh. Unknown at the time, a Russian-designed Kalashnikov or AK-47 was found next to the deceased militant. The others ran away from the scene. Surprisingly, there was no reaction from either the central or state government. No person in authority visited the crime scene. Everybody, including the heads of central intelligence agencies, ignored the attack to save their skin as all of them had failed to inform the government about Kashmiri boys crossing the LoC into PoK and returning with weapons. I was surprised why nobody took notice when my family and I had providentially survived a dastardly attack by about a dozen heavily armed militants.

BIG GAME OR INTELLIGENCE FAILURE

'Today, I speak of intelligence failure, but if I had to assign blame, I would honestly say that it was my fault,' admits my friend, A.S. Dulat, the then IB chief of the state.[40] In my first book, *Kashmir Intifada*, I had revealed that one sitting MLA had informed Prime Minister Rajiv Gandhi about the Kashmiri youth crossing the LoC and returning to the Valley with arms. The same MLA later told me that the prime minister had sent a note to the Director

---

[40]Dulat, Amarjit S., *A Life in the Shadows: A Memoir*, HarperCollins India, Gurugram, 2022, 43.

of Intelligence Bureau (DIB) Mr M.K. Narayanan who, under normal circumstances, would have obtained a report from his Srinagar office about the MLA's information. I am not sure if Dulat had been briefed about it by his predecessor; however, even before his Srinagar posting, he was stationed at the head office and working closely with Narayanan, had been was informed by the PM. The fact remains that the IB had information at the highest level, which, as per normal procedure, must have been shared with the Srinagar office. The silence of the agencies only points to a larger scheme involving the withholding of this vital intelligence.

THE IB'S PRIORITY

The IB's priority seemed to be keeping Dr Farooq Abdullah under surveillance. This duty was faithfully performed round the clock by Dulat. 'My mandate was to keep Farooq on our right side,' he says.[41] One can only guess whether this was a politically motivated game played by Rajiv Gandhi's government to suppress vital reports to push the state into a vortex of violence, score brownie points for future elections and disempower the people of the state. Security experts and readers are welcome to draw their own conclusions.

MILITANCY ERADICATED

Despite the continuous negative attitude of the ruling party at the centre, from September 1988 to October 1989, militancy was almost wiped out by the state police. We won the battle when out of the estimated 100 trained militants who had infiltrated the Valley, 72 were arrested along with their arms. The arrest

[41]Ibid. 174

of the remaining inactive lot was in the pipeline. Out of the wanted militants, only four actual combatants of the HAJY group (Hamid, Ashfaq, Javed and Yaseen) were active. Due to police pressure, even they were cooling their heels in PoK. Using investigative skills, detective abilities and public relations, the state police delivered results and fully controlled the situation without firing a single bullet. Peaceful conditions prevailed all across the Valley with a fairly large tourist footfall. The police had seized almost all the weaponry of the arrested militants, including Kalashnikov rifles, pistols, a huge quantity of ammunition, Chinese-made hand grenades, pencil bombs, anti-tank mines, rocket launchers and other lethal military stores. Kashmiri Pandits carried on with their daily life with no threat perception. The security forces also seemed to have been blissfully ignorant and unaware of armed infiltration at the LoC.

DIB'S VISIT

DIB M.K. Narayanan visited the state after the first militant attack and our subsequent operations to nab the perpetrators. He had a few one-on-one meetings with me. I briefed him about what all had happened and was likely to happen in the future. Before leaving for Delhi, he met with then DGP, Jeelani Pandit, in my presence. Apparently satisfied with the police operations, the DIB asked him if he required any assistance in tackling militancy. Pandit asked for an additional fleet of jeeps. Narayanan smiled and said, 'You require more Watalis than jeeps.' However, he immediately met the DG's demand. The Union cabinet secretary also visited the state and called me to the Lake View Guest House to discuss the fallout of militancy and the steps taken by the state police to nab all the militants. Practically no help was provided by the GoI.

RAJIV GANDHI'S VISIT

The suppression of prior information about militancy may have been a big game. Prime Minister Rajiv Gandhi, on his visit to Srinagar, did not allow journalists to record videos or take pictures while he was examining large quantities of arms and other lethal weapons seized by the state police. Was the state pushed into a vortex of militancy for political gains?

SECURITY COMPROMISED

Had the army also been taken on board by political bosses to prolong militancy? They were in denial about armed infiltration till mid-1989, as argued by GOC 19 Division Major General Mankotia and his formation commanders when I addressed an event organized by them at their Headquarters. How could they be unaware when they were supposed to guard the LoC? Was it a larger agenda they were hiding?

Meanwhile, Governor Jagmohan (during his first term) convened a meeting at Raj Bhavan which I also attended. CM Farooq Abdullah was also there, besides the top brass of the army, paramilitary forces and intelligence agencies. Dulat might also have been present. After all the seniors gave their assessment, the governor asked for my views. I informed him that militancy was fully controlled by the state police and that the Valley would soon be free from militancy provided the army effectively sealed the LoC to prevent further incursions. Surprisingly, the senior army general present there declared that that was not possible. I retaliated and told him, 'In that case we are betraying the nation. The people in the country believe that our borders are impregnable as our mighty army does not even allow a crow to fly in.' To the general's discomfort, I disclosed that the troops guarding the LoC were getting sizeable bribes to allow the militants to cross over to our side with arms. Though my frank statement provoked a protest by the general and unpleasantness in the meeting, Governor Jagmohan supported my point of view that unless the LoC was sealed, militancy would continue. In retrospect, I feel that the army's inaction at the border could have been aimed at allowing the situation to deteriorate to provide the GoI with an excuse to promulgate the draconian Armed Forces [Special Powers] Act (AFSPA), a demand long opposed by the state government.

ACTION PLAN

Once the army put their hands up, I drafted an action plan to establish border outposts (BOPs) manned by the local police in villages adjacent to the LoC to detect infiltration and arrest armed militants. To establish BOPs, I requested for only two Central Reserve Police Force companies which would replace and relieve the J&K police from static guard duties. A copy of my action plan was handed over to the joint secretary of the Ministry of Home Affairs, GoI, who, post the eradication of militancy, paid monthly visits to the Valley to interact with me and my officers in border districts. With a lot of anguish, I record that I was deprived of this minuscule number of men despite promises made by the joint secretary. The GoI did not provide the two requisitioned companies till I prematurely hung up my boots in October 1989. In hindsight, I feel that it was a deliberate attempt to sabotage my proposal, probably to allow militancy to escalate for political gains.

LATER DISCLOSURES

After hanging up my boots, while playing a round of golf at the BSF Golf Course in Jammu, I was told by retired Lieutenant General P.S. Vadhera, who was chief of staff of Northern Command during the crucial period, that the responsibility of guarding the LoC had been a controversial issue for a long time between the army and the BSF, particularly during 1987–89. Furthermore, General Vadhera plainly told me that borders could not be secured unless the army was empowered under AFSPA. With this logic, I told him that AFSPA should have then been enforced all along the Indo-Pak border as well as in the rest of the country. This again seems to have been the reason for the army to allow armed militants to infiltrate: to coerce the state government into applying AFSPA and thereafter take the front seat in addressing the militancy situation. I could not digest this argument and told General Vadhera as much. Why did the army require special powers at the border when guarding it was their basic duty? It seems that the GoI had also tried to escalate militancy to justify the application of AFSPA, which had been a permanent demand of the army even during peacetime in the Valley. Under the guise of this draconian law, they wanted absolute power to govern the state at grassroots level. Therefore, one may reasonably conclude that while allowing militancy to escalate, the army must have been in the loop. Otherwise, one cannot comprehend any ignorance on their part regarding the crossing and recrossing of Kashmiri youth with arms with impunity.

MILITARY OPTION

With the battle won and the situation completely normalized, J&K Police had the upper hand. Only a final goal remained to be scored when a sudden policy clash changed the entire operational scenario. Though the battle against militancy was won by the state police, Home Minister Buta Singh, without any rhyme or reason, decided to exercise the military option and hand over operational control to central forces. As a result, in mid-1989, the country was allowed to be sucked into a vortex of perpetual armed conflict within Jammu and Kashmir. Moreover, with the exercise of this erroneous military option, the battle won by the state police against militancy was lost to the Congress government at the centre. Wasn't this a calculate manoeuvre aimed at prolonging the agony of the people of the country, particularly those of J&K, for political gains? Aren't Indians entitled to know why this game was played? However, this action of the Congress government led me to resign as I could not afford to play second fiddle while dealing with this situation. I could not allow the gun to rest on my shoulder while the central forces pulled the trigger.

RUBAIYA SAYEED

Shortly after I resigned in October 1989, Rubaiya Sayeed, the daughter of Mufti Mohammad Sayeed, the home minister of India, was allegedly kidnapped on 8 December 1989 by JKLF militants, who demanded the release of five leading JKLF commanders arrested during my tenure. I had already moved to Jammu after taking over my assignment as a member of the Public Service Commission. Moosa Raza, the chief secretary of the state, was made the chief negotiator by the central government. He reported the progress to Cabinet Secretary T.N. Seshan.

We now have available a stark revelation, an authentic version, by none other than Moosa Raza. Making vital disclosures in his book, Moosa Raza writes[42]:

> I received a call from the cabinet secretary at 1.30 a.m. on 13 December. 'This is the cabinet secretary of the GoI, TN Seshan, speaking to the chief secretary of the state of Jammu and Kashmir, Mr Moosa Raza. I am speaking from the chamber of the prime minister of India. The GoI desires the state government to note that it is their undiluted responsibility to ensure the safe release of the hostage without any injury to her, and we expect that all actions you take will be consistent with this requirement'.

Reading between the lines, it was a stern warning delivered loud and clear to the state government to ensure Rubaiya's safe recovery at any cost, even if it meant releasing the five militants demanded by the kidnappers. Failure to comply could lead to the dismissal of the state government, which had already been conveyed to Dr Farooq by the ministerial group headed by Mr I.K. Gujral.

Referring to his post-retirement conversation with Seshan, Moosa Raza writes, 'I asked him, "I have always wondered about the sudden change in your approach when you dictated that ultimatum to me on the morning of 13 December. What was the reason for that?" "The game was much bigger," he said with a sardonic smile. "The target was much higher." "And what was that?" I asked.' Moosa Raza avoids revealing what Seshan told him by simply saying, 'His reply is a story for another day.' He further writes that later, DIB M.K. Narayanan also gave him more or less the same reply.[43]

By swapping Rubaiya with the jailed militants, the security scenario of the Valley changed abruptly. Even pro-Pakistan

---

[42]Raza, Moosa, *Kashmir: Land of Regrets*, Context, New Delhi, 2019, 196.
[43]Ibid.

leaders and the general public were sceptical about the existence of any armed struggle for freedom. Victory processions of azadi erupted all over the Valley. The release of the arrested militants was considered a victory of 'Kashmiri freedom fighters'. The wiped-out militancy got a boost; it was revived and converted into a popular armed uprising for azadi. One can only speculate about the larger motives behind this exchange but nothing can be stated with certainty. Was it collusion between the kidnappers and the kidnapped? Was it bait to militants to encourage them to resume their activities with more zeal? I can't say with certainty. However, I wonder why the GoI had categorically warned the state government to ensure her safe release, which could not be achieved without releasing the jailed militants. Further, one can't imagine why the daughter of the home minister of India was freely moving in public transport without any security. The induction of personal negotiators by Mufti for his daughter's release while ignoring the chief secretary of the state, official interlocutor and intelligence apparatus of the GoI available in Srinagar strengthens suspicions about a hidden agenda that he did not want leaked to the state government. The people of the country have the right to know what was the big game was and what was the higher target. One of the objectives could have been to find an excuse to remove Dr Farooq's government. It could also have been to create a situation to justify the promulgation of draconian laws like the Disturbed Areas Act and AFSPA, which the state government had always resisted. Mufti had moved a bill in Parliament in mid-1990 for the application of AFSPA to the Valley. Nothing can be said with certainty unless a proper inquiry commission is appointed with a clear mandate to uncover the truth.

The stern midnight warning to Moosa Raza, coupled with the threat of dismissal to Dr Abdullah by the visiting ministerial group led by I.K. Gujral, left the state government with no choice but to release the militants against Dr Farooq's wishes. These events surely point to a hidden agenda engineered at the cost of national security by the home minister, with V.P. Singh, the Raja of Manda, at the helm. Needless to say, Rubaiya's release renewed the already eradicated militancy and converted it into a conflagration, resulting in the continued bleeding of paradise on earth to this day.

JAGMOHAN'S OMINOUS APPEARANCE

After exchanging the militants for Rubaiya Sayeed, the centre suddenly decided to replace Governor General K.V. Krishna Rao. Accordingly, a panel of four names was reportedly sent to CM Dr Farooq, which included the name of Naresh Chandra, a thorough gentleman, hardened bureaucrat and later a cabinet secretary. Dr Farooq is believed to have given his consent to all the names. However, he warned the centre not to send Jagmohan, even though his name did not feature in the panel. It is believed that no one in the state bureaucracy or at the centre supported Jagmohan's appointment. He was believed to have been sent as the governor of the state only on Mufti's recommendation, to push Dr Farooq to resign. With Jagmohan's nomination, Dr Farooq put in his papers with Governor General Krishna Rao. Accordingly, the state came under governor's rule, which was another big game to further destabilize the state.[44]

JAGMOHAN'S AGENDA EXPOSED

Jagmohan, instead of imposing restrictions to buy time to stabilize his position and save citizens' life and property, allowed

---

[44]Raza, Moosa, *Kashmir: Land of Regrets*, Context, New Delhi, 2019.

azadi processions to move freely, thereby putting them in the line of security forces' fire. In the process, hundreds of peaceful, unarmed demonstrators were killed.

LOC THROWN OPEN

A senior IAS officer exposed to me that Jagmohan threw open the LoC and allowed the free movement of Kashmiris into PoK, knowing that they would return after being trained and with arms. A sovereign country allowing its own citizens' entry into enemy territory is unheard of in history. Could this be done without the knowledge and orders of the home minister or prime minister? The logic of this decision points to political motives.

It is believed that Mufti and Jagmohan were on the same page since the latter's appointment as governor. A shocking revelation was made to me in the winter of 2020 by a reliable source, a retired chief secretary-level officer of the state, when he called on me in Jammu. While recalling past events, I asked him why Kashmiri youth were allowed to go to PoK during his tenure. He said it was allowed by Jagmohan under the orders of Home Minister Mufti Mohammad Sayeed. According to him, Jagmohan had admitted as much in 1990 in a meeting of Hindu officers convened by him. In the meeting, Mr. Gupta, an IAS cadre officer of the state who hailed from Himachal Pradesh, had asked Jagmohan why he had allowed Kashmiri youth to cross over to PoK without restrictions. 'Mufti asked me to let the Kashmiri youth cross into PoK as all of them were miscreants,' he is said to have replied. What a bone-chilling message for the citizens of a democratic country. The decision by the Mufti–Jagmohan duo was like a medieval punishment to the citizens of the Valley. This event also must have substantially increased the human resources available for militancy sponsors to continue causing violence and unrest in the state.

EXODUS OF KASHMIRI PANDITS

The exodus of Kashmiri Pandits was also a big game triggered on 19 January 1990, with Jagmohan's advent. According to my knowledge, no Kashmiri Pandit had migrated during Dr Farooq's regime. Militants targeted Kashmiri Pandits and pro-India Muslims, indicating that the idea of India was under attack, not a community. The pattern of killings clearly proves my findings. I believe that the present generation of Kashmiri Pandits, who are well settled in other parts of the country and in other countries, are not interested in returning. Those who had been provided employment under PM Manmohan Singh's employment package are now refusing to serve in the Valley because of the killing of some Kashmiri Pandit employees in 2022, that is, even after the abrogation of the special status of the state in 2019.

According to Dr Farooq, this exodus was the biggest betrayal of Kashmiri Pandits by Jagmohan, who used their victimhood for political gains.[45]

IKHWAN GAME

In 2002–03, the counterinsurgency situation became tough for the Hizb-ul-Mujahideen. Their rank and file and most of their mentors, on-ground and underground workers were brutally wiped out by a reneged sister outfit, Ikhwan-ul-Muslimeen, led by the notorious armed militant Mohammad Yusuf Parray, aka Kuka Parray, a Kashmiri folk singer from Hajin Sonawari in

[45]'Ex-J&K Guv Jagmohan Put Kashmiri Pandits in Buses, Said They'd Be Brought Back in 2 Months: Farooq Abdullah', *India Today*, 22 March 2022, https://www.indiatoday.in/india/story/jammu-kashmir-governor-jagmohan-kashmiri-pandits-farooq-abdullah-kashmir-files-1928035-2022-03-22. Accessed on 14 February 2024.

Bandipore district. This ruthless and desperate outfit made the lives of the common people hell when they were converted into a formidable counterinsurgent group and had free rein to kill whoever they wanted. The heinous crimes committed by him and his gang are unlike the counterinsurgency in any country. Aged and respectable people were cruelly tortured and killed by being hanged on lamp posts. People were dragged through the streets like dead dogs.

In south Kashmir, a similar group was patronized by the security forces, and some of them were even recruited into the Territorial Army. The Hizb-ul-Mujahideen was the worst-hit militant organization and could not be revived thereafter. Kuka Parray even contested the 1996 state assembly elections when the political process was revived after Dr Farooq Abdullah's return from London. The Ikhwanis resorted to coercion and forced people to vote for Kuka Parray at gunpoint. Kuka Parray was elected under the banner of his own political party: Awami League. Ultimately, when on his way to inaugurate a cricket match on 13 September 2003, Kuka Parray was killed by some militants. With his death, his gang was eradicated and the people got freedom from the barbarism of the Ikhwanis. The ISI cannot escape blame for arming such criminal elements. Although this was a counterinsurgency operation, the army cannot escape accountability for the heinous crimes committed by this notorious group.

FOREIGN MILITANTS

To infuse fresh blood into their project, the ISI played another big game when they, for the first time, pushed Pakistani nationals, called 'foreign militants', into the Valley. These militants were products of radical Islamic madrasas operating in Pakistan, mostly in west Punjab. Some of them were battle-hardened Mujahideen who had fought in Afghanistan against Russian occupation. Moulana Azhar Masood launched Jaish-e-Mohammad and vowed to fight the Indian state in Kashmir. Jamaat-ud-Dawa, headed by Hafiz Sayed, was another extremist Islamic organization, with its militant outfit Lashkar-e-Taiba, that pushed their militants into the Valley. This Mulla–ISI nexus ultimately boomeranged, resulting in dastardly terrorist attacks by radicalized Islamist groups within Pakistan itself.

Pakistan reportedly lost more than 80,000 of troops to terrorism, in addition to thousands of innocent civilians. Even General Musharraf, the then dictator president of Pakistan, was attacked twice but escaped unhurt. By 2004–05, Kashmir militancy came to be completely controlled by the ISI–Lashkar-e-Taiba–Jaish-e-Mohammad consortium that had their offices in Pakistan. Suicide bombing in Kashmir was introduced by the foreign militants of these organizations. The Pakistan-based Jaish-e-Mohammad took responsibility for major terrorist attacks, such as the Pulwama suicide attack wherein 42 officers of the Central Reserve Police Force were killed. Similarly, in the past, Lashkar-e-Taiba has claimed responsibility for other operations in the Valley.

LOCAL YOUTH RADICALIZED

With the induction of Pakistani Islamist militants into the Valley, the teenage recruits of militancy were brainwashed about the afterlife advantages of their martyrdom. The main victims of this radicalization were the youth belonging to families that had a JI background, mostly in south Kashmir. Thus, by 2010, Burhan Wani became the poster boy of jihad in Kashmir, particularly in the southern parts. After his death in 2016, radicalized militancy was consolidated, primarily in the Jamaat pockets of south Kashmir. Innocent teenage boys are lured into militancy after a few days of training. Within days, they get consumed in this gory game of blood and fire. From January to June 2020 alone, about 100 such boys were killed in various encounters within the Valley, especially in south Kashmir.

LONE'S SOMERSAULT

We have seen Abdul Ghani Lone playing a big game by collaborating with General Zia-ul-Haq to initiate an armed uprising in the Valley. The Zia–Lone project was ab initio deceptive, as Lone also did a somersault. Around 2000, with unprecedented death and destruction in the state, his latest project was to appear as chief minister during the National Democratic Alliance rule headed by Prime Minister Atal Bihari Vajpayee at the centre. He had already established contacts with the GoI through a veteran journalist, late R.K. Mishra. I have seen him with Mishra in New Delhi many times. Lone even consulted me about the modalities of taking over as chief minister. Readers may recall that back in around 1966, when he was a deputy minister in the Sadiq government, in a statement in Mumbai, he advocated for the abrogation of Article 370 of the Constitution. Ideologically, he was neither pro-Pakistani nor in favour of azadi.

VAJPAYEE'S GAME

In an attempt to decimate the NC for daring to pass an autonomy resolution in the assembly, Prime Minister Vajpayee created the PDP with the help of his intelligence chief Ajit Doval. Nevertheless, the NC refused to get decimated and again rose to power.

PAKISTAN ARMY RADICALIZED

The Afghan war against the Union of Soviet Socialist Republics brought Pakistan into the arena of conflict and reportedly made it a haven for international Islamic terrorists. This development, coupled with the seeds of conflict sown by Zia-ul-Haq, may have led to radicalization seeping deep into the Pakistan Army too. They came closer to Al-Qaeda and other such radical organizations from within and outside Pakistan. That is how radicalized militancy was introduced to Kashmiri militants with the induction of foreign militants. Via the ISI, the Pakistan Army also became a party to the struggle inside Kashmir, helping train and equip Islamist fighters and militants who infiltrated and injected themselves into the battle between Kashmiris and the huge Indian military and paramilitary force that was sent to quell the insurgency in Kashmir.[46] It is believed the Lashkar-e-Taiba and Jaish-e-Mohammad are fighting Indian forces in Kashmir not for the liberation of Kashmir but as a global jihad against infidels worldwide.

ISIS FLAGS

In an attempt to mislead the world, ISIS flags were displayed on a few occasions during anti-India demonstrations in downtown Srinagar. It is firmly believed that the ISIS had no presence in the Valley and that they were not even remotely connected with the militancy going on in the state since 1988. The hoisting of an ISIS flag by stone pelters on the parapet of Jamia Masjid with

---

[46]Ahmed, Khaled, 'Shuja Nawaz's New Book Explores Differences Between Pakistan Army and Radical Elements', *The Indian Express*, 1 February 2020, https://indianexpress.com/article/opinion/columns/khaled-ahmed-pakistan-military-us-india-relations-6244973/. Accessed on 2 January 2024.

their shoes on, thereby desecrating the mosque, proves it was a big game because even a non-Muslim would not commit such a crime of desecration. This was a crude game only to defame Kashmiris as votaries of the ISIS.

OPERATION P 10

A scheme was launched by a senior intelligence doyen, who roped in a young separatist leader and promised 10 seats for his party if he agreed to field his candidates in the 2002 state elections. This separatist leader, whom I knew very well, sought my advice. I clearly told him that no one sitting in the corridors of power, much less his intelligence friend, could make any of his proxy candidates win. However, he seemed very enthusiastic to field his 10 proxy candidates as advised by his intelligence boss, who codenamed this arrangement as Operation P 10. The intelligence boss made huge financial resources available. All the P 10 candidates, except one, lost. In reality, Operation P 10 was launched by the intelligence boss to squeeze the NC's vote share in line with Vajpayee's policy of keeping them away from power. Otherwise, they would have surely won a few more seats against the PDP and formed the government. The big game was exposed as they only wanted to decimate the NC by strengthening the PDP. Nobody was interested in the victory of the separatist leader's candidates. The lone wining P 10 candidate was, however, inducted as a cabinet minister in the first Mufti government as a reward by the intelligence boss.

LONE'S TRAGIC END

Temperamentally, Lone was not someone who could be dictated too long. Only a few days after his return from Dubai, after meeting the ISI bosses, he was shot dead in a precision attack by unknown gunmen at Eidgah, Srinagar, on 21 May 2002, while participating in the martyrdom anniversary of Mirwaiz Moulana Mohammad Farooq. Levy and Scott-Clark, in *Spy Stories: Inside the Secret World of ISI and RAW*, note[47]:

> One leader singled out for scolding by the ISI was Abdul Ghani Lone [...] In April 2002, Hurriyat leader Abdul Ghani Lone had visited Dubai on his way to Pakistan. He met with allies, including the Mirwaiz Umar Farooq, and debated Pakistan by calling for all armed fighters to quit.
>
> Lone had had quite a *tête-à-tête* with the intelligence chief, General (Ehsan) Ul-Haq, during which Lone complained bitterly about the ISI's insensitivity in handling Hurriyat and attacked an officer famous as Brigadier Abdullah. General Ul-Haq listened and got irritated. Lone was a client and required deft handling [...] Pakistan needed peace in the Valley to keep its US pact, but if Pakistani assets backed an Indian truce, it would look like surrender, something the ISI could not stomach. Shortly after Lone's visit, an 'Abdullah' was shunted off the Kashmir desk [...] On May 20, 2002, veteran Lone was shot dead at an open-air rally in Srinagar. [...] The planner was the vengeful ISI Brigadier 'Abdullah' whom Lone had got fired.

With his death, Lone's big game to become chief minister of the state was aborted.

While recording the big games, I realized that they were a subject matter for a full volume. I selected only a few to inform the readers about what was happening behind the scenes to

---

[47]Levy, Adrian, and Cathy Scott-Clark, *Spy Stories: Inside the Secret World of ISI and RAW*, Juggernaut, New Delhi, 2021, 61, 105–07

destabilize the state for political power. The readers may appreciate that notwithstanding playing big games, those in power have failed to eradicate militancy for the last three decades. The battle won by the state police back in 1989 has been lost with a colossal loss of life and national resources.

Epilogue

Initially, the Bharatiya Janata Party government seemed to be interested in having friendly relations with Pakistan, which could have ultimately lead to the permanent settlement of the Kashmir problem. The positivity was indicated by the presence of Pakistani Prime Minister Nawaz Sharif as a prominent leader among the distinguished guests at Prime Minister Modi's oath-taking ceremony. Later, Prime Minister Modi's surprise landing at Lahore was an unprecedented friendly gesture to congratulate Prime Minister Nawaz Sharif on his grandson's marriage. It seems that the ISI was not in the loop, as unfortunately, in response to Prime Minister Modi's peace gesture, the Indian Air Force base at Pathankot was attacked by Pakistani terrorists. Obviously, this was done by one of the ISI-patronized hardcore Islamic groups based in Pakistan. Thereafter, in a drastic policy shift, the Indian government stopped all peace overtures with Pakistan. Since then, India has not shown any inclination to even discuss the possibility of resuming dialogue with Pakistan. Subsequent events, particularly the Pulwama attack, have further deteriorated relations, culminating in a warlike situation between the two countries on 29 September 2016.

Suddenly, on 25 February 2021, the whiff of a spring breeze appeared on the horizon, particularly for the border residents of the state, when the Directors General of Military Operations of both countries declared a ceasefire along the LoC and the international border of the state. Though nothing more was disclosed, a push by some invisible powers must have been responsible for this pleasant surprise. The peace process was not carried further to strengthen ties. With this pleasant thaw, the central government could announce a unilateral ceasefire and declare amnesty for the gun-wielding Kashmiri youth to pave the way for their meaningful rehabilitation and peace.

The ceasefire of 25 February began with positive vibes. Let us hope that the process ultimately leads to the final settlement of the Kashmir dispute to the satisfaction of both countries and the people living in the five regions of the erstwhile undivided state: Jammu, Kashmir, Ladakh–Kargil, PoK and Gilgit–Baltistan. I am sure that once this longstanding issue is finally resolved, the prime ministers of both countries will be eligible for the Nobel Peace Prize. Their names will be written in golden letters with the settlement of the Kashmir dispute. The threat of a nuclear war between the two countries will be averted, and valuable resources eaten up by the defence budgets of both countries can instead be diverted to poverty alleviation programmes, thereby leading to the eradication of poverty, hunger and deprivation.

Bibliography

Abullah, Sheikh Mohmmad, *The Blazing Chinar*, Gulshan Books, Srinagar, 2013.

Ahmad, Mohammad Zafar, *Payam-e-Hurriyat*, Mehdi Ali Khan, Allahabad, 1940.

Asad, Muhammad Saeed, *Deewanon Pe Kya Guzri*, National Institute of Kashmir Studies, Mirpur, 2012.

Dulat, Amarjit S, *A Life in the Shadows: A Memoir*, HarperCollins India, Gurugram, 2022.

Dulat, Amarjit S., and Aditya Sinha, *Kashmir: The Vajpayee Years*, HarperCollins India, Gurugram, 2015.

Khan, Sardar Ibrahim, *The Kashmir Saga*, Verinag Publishers, Mirpur, 1965.

Levy, Adrian, and Cathy Scott-Clark, *Spy Stories: Inside the Secret World of ISI and RAW*, Juggernaut, New Delhi, 2021.

Raza, Moosa, *Kashmir: Land of Regrets*, Westland Publications, New Delhi, 2019.

Reidel, Bruce, *JFK's Forgotten Crisis: Tibet, the CIA, and the Sino-Indian War*, HarperCollins India, Gurugram, 2016.

Saraf, Muhammad Y., *Kashmiris Fight for Freedom, Vol. 2 (1947–1978)*, Ferozsons, Lahore, 1979.

Watali, Ali M., *Kashmir Intifada*, Gulshan Books, Srinagar, 2017.

Abbreviations

AFSPA	Armed Forces (Special Powers) Act
BSF	Border Security Force
CFL	Ceasefire Line
CI	Counter Intelligence
CID	Crime Investigation Department
CJI	Chief Justice of India
CM	Chief Minister
CrPC	Code of Criminal Procedure
DC	Deputy Commissioner
DGP	Director General of Police
DIB	Director Intelligence Bureau
DIG	Deputy Inspector General of Police
E&IMCO	Egress and Internal Movement Control Ordinance
GMC	Government Medical College, Srinagar
GOC	General Officer Commanding
GoI	Government of India
HC	High Commissioner
HAJY	Hamid, Ishfaq, Javed and Yaseen
IB	Intelligence Bureau
IGP	Inspector General of Police
IO	Investigating Officer
ISI	Inter-Services Intelligence
JI	Jamaat-e-Islami
JIC	Joint Interrogation Centre
JKLF	Jammu Kashmir Liberation Front
KIC	Kashmir Independence Committee

LoC	Line of Control
MLA	Member of Legislative Assembly
MUF	Muslim United Front
NC	National Conference
NCC	National Cadet Corps
NLF	National Liberation Front
PAF	Pakistan Air Force
PCR	Police Control Room
PF	Plebiscite Front
PHC	Pakistan High Commission, New Delhi
PoK	Pakistan-occupied Kashmir
POWs	Prisoners of War
REC	Regional Engineering College, Srinagar
RUA	Rahmat Ulahi Allie
SHO	Station House Officer
SOP	Standard Operating Procedure
SP	Superintendent of Police
SRC	Students' Revolutionary Council
SS	Special Staff
SSP	Senior Superintendent of Police
UNSC	United Nations Security Council